Historical Atlas
of the Great Khans:
Mongol Wars and Conquests
1160-1304

ISBN 978-1986729611

Printed by Create Space
www.createspace.com

Historical Atlas
of the Great Khans:
Mongol Wars and Conquests
1160-1304

John Carl Nelson

A World History Maps Book ™

Preface

A handful of times in the history of the world, a previously obscure people living on the fringes of civilization, burst upon the scene and within a short time changed the course of history. One of the most spectacular of these peoples were the Mongols of the Thirteenth Century. Within the space of one lifetime, they were unified and forged into an invincible war machine. Within another generation, this force went on to conquer half of the civilized world, and brought the ends of Eurasia into contact with one another. Much that shapes our world today is a result of these contacts.

This feat was essentially the work of one man. His name was Temujin and he became known far and wide as Chinggis Khan. His sons carried on his work and the force he released upon the world would not stop until his grandsons began to fight with one another.

This book tells the story of the Mongol Wars and Conquests by means of a series of maps. Most of the time the Mongol Conquests are shown by a single map, or at most four or five maps. This atlas will go into much greater detail with as many maps as necessary to tell the complete story. Breaking the narrative into smaller, more discrete segments, makes it more understandable.

I have been interested in the Mongols ever since reading Harold Lamb's biography of Chinggis Khan back in high school. Over the years, I have sometimes been frustrated, when reading about the Mongols, by the lack of maps where I could follow the narrative in some detail. I have also noticed that sometimes the narratives don't make much sense when I try to plot things out on a map. The few maps that are shown in general works seldom show any details. This book is an attempt to sort it all out for myself and to share what I have learned with others. The source information itself is sometimes missing, limited, or inconsistent. But I hope my maps are a step in the right direction and will be useful to others. I have learned a great deal in the process of writing this book, but one of the important thing I have learned is how much remains to be explored in detail.

The sources I have used are almost exclusively in English. I was only able to read names in Chinese historical atlases and chronologies. The details of early years are mostly based on Igor de Rachewiltz's translation of the *Secret History* and Bazargur's atlas. The wars with Xixia and Jin China are covered in Desmond Martin's work. The recent book by Carl Sverdrup was acquired too late to incorporate all his details, but I did redraw one map where there were major differences and added a few things to some other maps. A complete incorporation of this work may require a second edition. For the wars in the west I relied a lot on the Cambridge Histories and McLynn's biography. The wars with Song China do not have a thorough study. Except for Bayan's biography, translated by Francis Cleves, I primarily used the Chinese atlases and chronologies. The wars in Central Asia are covered in some detail by Biran and Dicosimo. Many other works were consulted as noted, but this is not a work of exhaustive scholarship.

I have been interested in maps, particularly historical maps, for a long time. In 1997, I set out on a project to develop one map for every year for the past 5,000 years. This started out because I was looking for consistent maps that I could use in my family history web site. I couldn't find what I wanted and thought that if I wanted this, other people might want it too. This led to worldhistorymaps.com and a set of interactive historical atlases on CD-ROM and DVD-ROM, and now books and mobile apps.

John Carl Nelson, 2018

Contents

Introduction

The goal of this book is to present a story of how the Mongols became united and went on to conquer much of Eurasia. The story is told by a series of maps.

The places, borders, and itineraries of 800 years ago cannot possibly be known with GPS accuracy. Many of the dates are also not known with certainty, especially in the early years. The sources even do not agree on the sequence of some events. This should be considered when reading the maps, since placing a marker or drawing a line on a map tends to imply more exact knowledge than there is. Borders especially should be taken as generalizations only. The courses of rivers and the shape of mountain ranges frequently dictate the routes that must be used. In cases of conflicting or limited information, I have chosen what makes most sense to me.

This is strictly a military and political atlas. It is about what, where, and when, not how or why.

The atlas is arranged chronologically with chapters for each of the Great Khans, plus an additional first chapter for Temujin before he became Chinggis Khan.

Each chapter starts with a map of the countries and peoples of the Old World and a brief description or chronology grouped by regions. The chronologies explain the changes since the previous map.

Following this introduction to the chapter, individual maps showing specific events are arranged in chronological order. With each map there is a brief description of the events. Each map also has an insert showing its location in the wider world.

Following the chapters is a detailed chronological index of events. Due to uncertainty, most events do not have exact dates. Events are listed sequentially within years. Following the chronology are bibliography, footnotes, and an index. The footnotes may contain additional comments for the maps as well as references, and in some cases more information about events. The comprehensive name and subject index at the end includes many details about individuals and places.

The following symbols are used on the maps.

Red is for actions by the Khan's forces or allies. Blue is for enemies. Black is for others or indecisive battles. Purple is for Mongol civil wars after 1259. Labels for movements are always on the right hand side of the path.

Military Moves

————▶   ————▶   ————▶   ————▶

Military Retreats

— — —▶   — — —▶   — — —▶   — — —▶

Non-military Moves

- - - - -▶   - - - - -▶   - - - - -▶   - - - - -▶

Battles won or cities captured.   ×   ×   ×   ×

Cities surrendered.   +   +   +   +

Cities under siege .   ⊙

Fortified Positions   ▢

Capital Cities   ☆

Other Cities   ○

Other Places   ▫

Cities in a single country all have the same interior color.

Independent countries and tribes

Xixia, Onguds

Subordinate countries and tribes

(Xixia), (Onguds)

A note on spelling. The romanization of foreign names is a difficult problem. Many countries have adopted new systems in recent years, but a lot of the sources used the older systems. I have tried to conform to the most current usage as best I could. See the Indexes for more information.

Temujin, 1160 to 1206

Countries & Peoples – 1/1/1160

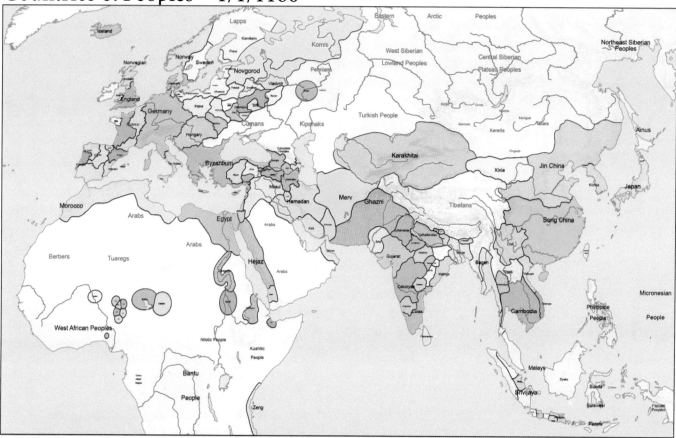

Africa: Bantu people inhabited most of Central Africa. They were expanding to the south and absorbing or replacing other Central African peoples. North of the Bantus were Nilotic and Kushitic people. In the Sahel from west to east were Songhai, the several Hausa states, Kanem and Bornu, three Christian Kingdoms, and Muslim Adal. West African people lived in the rain forest further south; Berbers and Tuaregs lived in the Sahara. Morocco held the Mediterranean Coast.

Western Europe: Morocco had also expanded into Spain, conquering most of the Muslim kingdoms and pushing the Christian kingdoms back. Most of France was controlled by Plantagenet England. The Hohenstaufen Emperor of Germany was trying to restore imperial power. Italian cities and the Papacy resisted. The Nordic kingdoms and Poland were expanding at the expense of the Baltic Tribes. Norway had established outposts in the North Atlantic. Hungary was the eastern limit of Western Christianity.

Eastern Europe: The Rus Principalities contended with one another for control of Kyyiv (Kiev). Novgorod in the north controlled the fur trade. The Comneni Emperors of Byzantium had partially restored its fortunes and had regained some land in Anatolia. They were threatened in the west.

Middle East: The Middle East was crowded with minor states which included the Crusader kingdoms along the coast. The Crusaders held Jerusalem and threatened Egypt. The Fatimid dynasty of Egypt was in decline. Further east the Seljuk empire had split up into four branches in 1155. Independent Ghazni had expanded into India.

Central Asia: The Western Steppe was dominated by the Cumans and Kipchaks. Further east were the Turkish People. The silk road was controlled by Karakhitai and Xixia. Some of the tribes of the Eastern Steppe had formed confederations but the Emperors of Jin China played them against each other. The Siberian Peoples were unknown to the outside world.

Eastern Asia: The Jin Dynasty had conquered North China in 1127. The Song Dynasty held on in Central and Southern China. This was still the most populous and richest country in the world. Korea was subordinate to Jin China. Japan was on the verge of civil war between the various military clans.

Southern Asia: In the north, Muslim rulers had gained a foothold. The contending Hindu kingdoms remained vulnerable. In the Deccan, the once dominant Calukyas were engulfed in civil war which also involved the neighboring once vassal kingdoms. The Colas dominated the far south.

South-Eastern Asia: Cambodia dominated the mainland but was in the midst of a chaotic period at this time. In the islands, the once powerful kingdom of Srivijaya had declined, as outlying regions became independent.

13

The Eastern Steppe, 1160

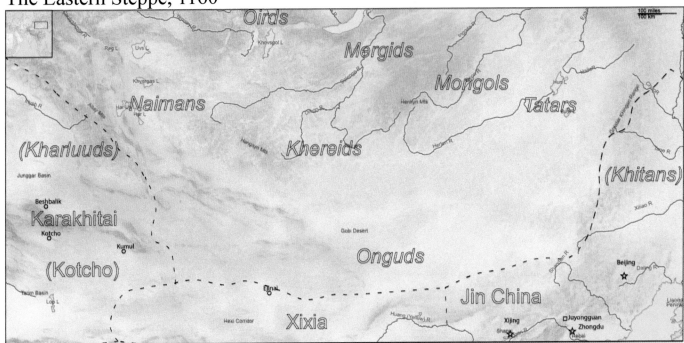

The Eastern Steppe World in the Twelfth Century was fragmented and unstable. Even in those tribes that had a recognized leader, such as the Naimans and Khereids, the hold of the leader was tenuous. Family groups and small clans frequently changed allegiance among larger units or individual leaders. The influence of Jin China was strong among the Tatars and Onguds. Tribes to the south had more access to trade with settled countries. Northern tribes were poorer.[1]

Temujin's Early Years, 1160 to 1170

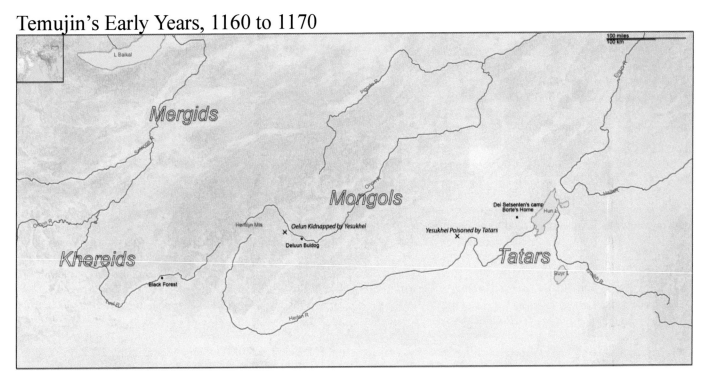

In 1161 or thereabouts, Yesukhei, leader of the Khiyad Mongol clan and sworn friend of Tooril of the Khereids, kidnapped Oelun from the Mergids for his second wife. The following year, Oelun's son was born at Deluun Buldog and given the name Temujin. When Temujin was 8, Yesukhei took his son to seek a wife. Temujin met Borte at the home of her father, Dei Setsenten. Dei Setsenten agreed to their marriage. Temujin was to stay there until they were married. Yesukhei was poisoned by Tatars on the way home, however, and Temujin returned home.[2]

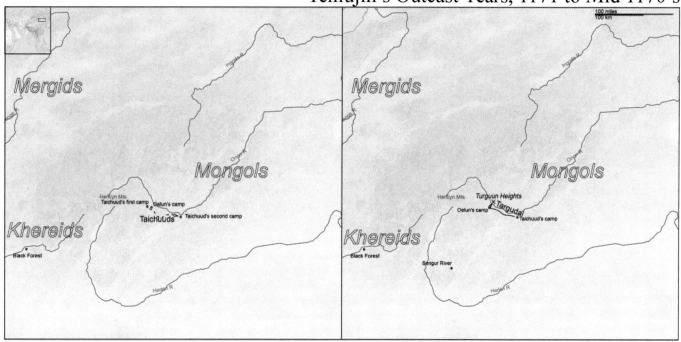

Following Yesukhei's death, his followers joined the Taichuud Mongol clan who abandoned Oelun and her family. At age 10, Temujin bonded with Jamukha. Later Temujin, and his brother Khasar, killed their older half-brother Begter. [3]

After this incident, Targudai, leader of the Taichuuds, captured Temujin at Turguun Heights and held him prisoner for some time. Temujin escaped with the help of the Taichuud family of Sorkhon Shar. [4]

Temujin Becomes Established, Mid 1170's to 1180

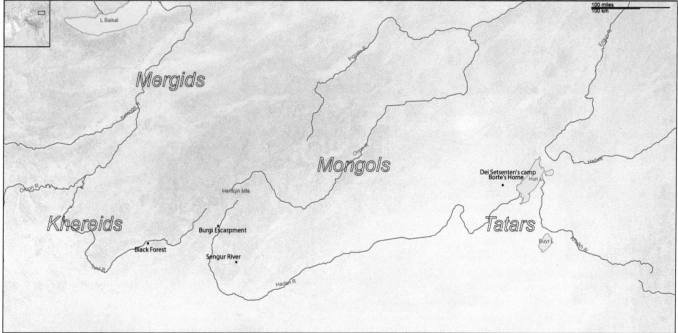

Once he escaped, Temujin and family established camp on the Sengur River. In the late 1170s, Temujin recovered stolen horses with the help of Boorchi. Boorchi then joined Temujin. Temujin moved their camp to the Burgi Escarpment on the Herlen River. Zelme joined Temujin. In 1180, Temujin traveled to claim Borte as his wife. After Borte returned with Temujin, he travelled to the camp of Tooril of the Khereids at the Black Forest. There he sought Tooril's patronage, based on Tooril's former sworn friendship with Yesukhei. Tooril agreed. [5]

Capture of Borte 1181

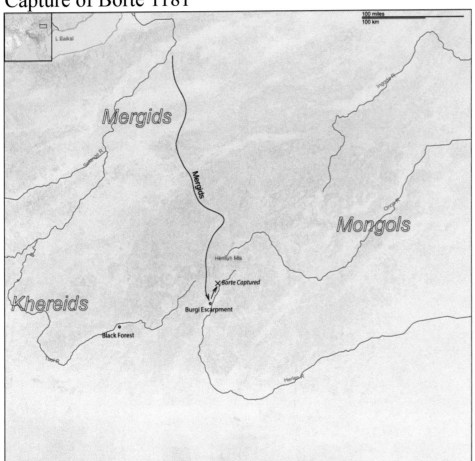

In 1181, Togtoa, Dayir Usun, and Darmala of the Mergids raided Temujin's camp and kidnapped Borte in revenge for the kidnapping of Oelun. Temujin asked Tooril and Jamukha for help. [6]

Rescue of Borte 1182

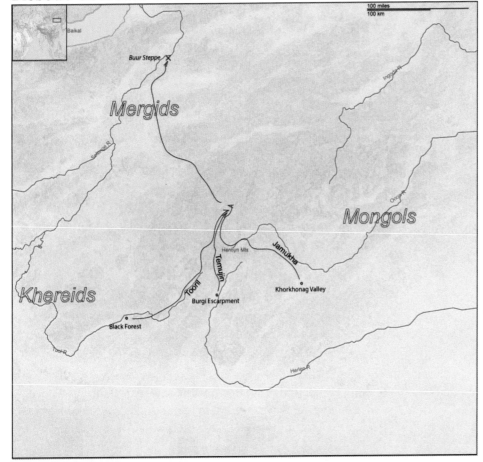

The following year Tooril, Jamukha, and Temujin joined forces to attack the Mergids and recover Borte. The combined force advanced into Mergid territory, defeated Togtoa at the Buur Steppe, and rescued Borte. They then split up, Tooril returned south while Temujin and Jamukha went west. Borte's first son, Zuchi, was born a short time later. [7]

After the rescue of Borte, Jamukha and Temujin returned and camped together in the Khorkhonag Valley. Two years later Temujin separated from Jamukha and established his own camp at Ayil Khargantad. Later, Temujin moved his camp to Koko Naur, and then to the Sengur River. Temujin attracted many followers over the next few years. His family also increased, son Tsagadai was born in 1183, and son Ogedei in 1186. In 1189, Temujin's followers hailed him as Khan of the Mongols. [8]

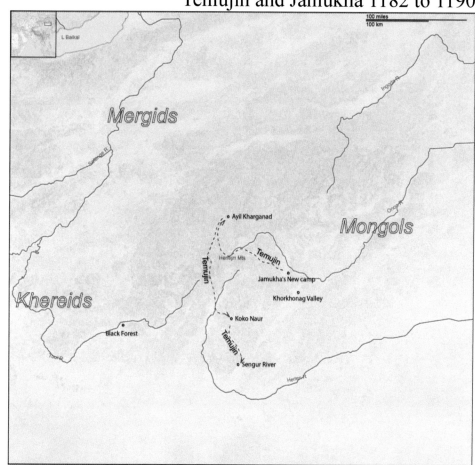

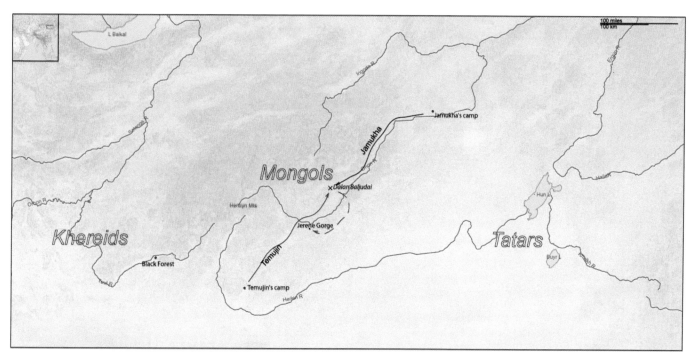

In 1190, Jamukha moved against Temujin. Temujin was warned and moved to engage him at Dalan Baljudai. Temujin was defeated and fled to Jerene Gorge. Temujin later returned home but continued to attract followers. [9]

War with the Tatars, 1196

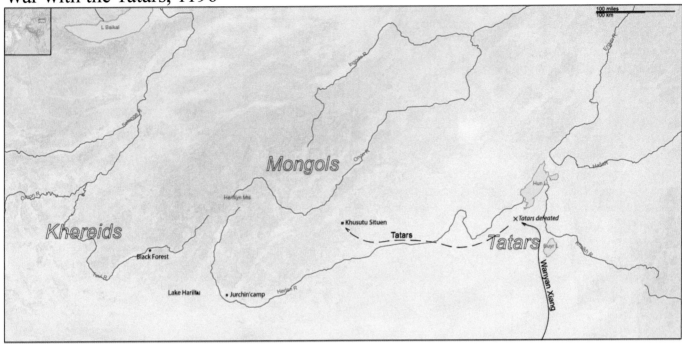

In 1196, Wanyan Xiang led a Jin expedition against some rebellious Tatars. The Tatars were defeated and retreated west, establishing a fortified position at Khusutu Situen. [10]

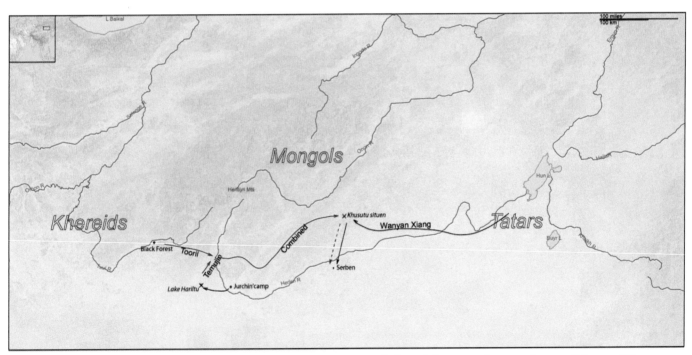

Temujin and Tooril moved to attack the Tatars from the west and defeated them at Khusutu Situen. Wanyan Xiang rewarded Tooril with the title of King and Temujin with the title of Commander. A boy, Shikhikhutug, was found in the Tatar camp and adopted by Oelun. While Temujin was away, the Jurchin Mongol clan attacked his camp. [11]

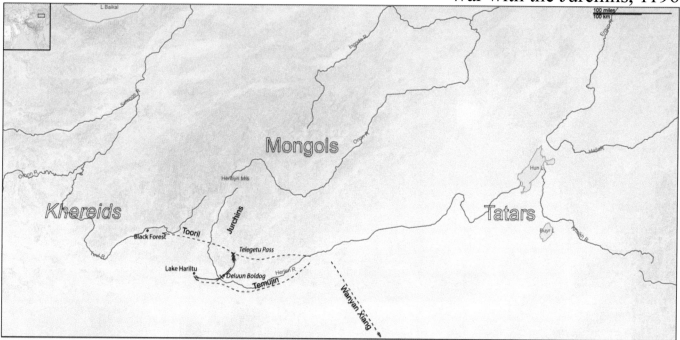

Temujin returned to find his camp had been attacked. He marched against the Jurchins and defeated them at Deluun Buldog. Some of the Jurchins fled but Temujin pursued them to the Telegetu Pass, where he defeated them again. Temujin absorbed the remaining Jurchins into his forces and established a new permanent base at Avarga, in their former territory. Mukhulai joined Temujin. [12]

War with Jamukha's Coalition, 1201

Jamukha formed a coalition of uncommitted Mongol clans, Tatars, Mergids, and the western tribes of Naimans and Oirds against Temujin. They proclaimed Jamukha as Universal Khan and set out to attack Temujin. Temujin was warned and summoned Tooril to his aid. Temujin and Tooril met Jamukha's forces at Kuyiten and defeated them. [13]

War with the Taichuuds, 1201

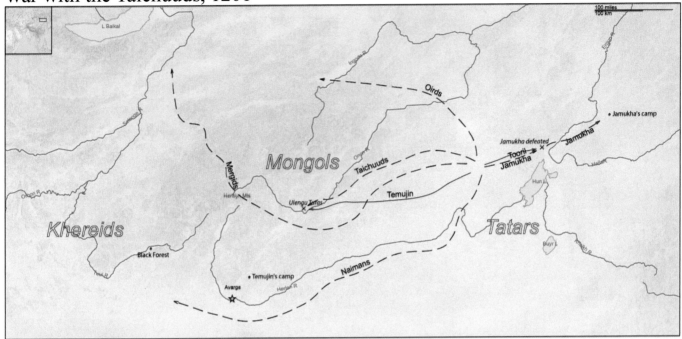

Jamukha and his allies fled in all directions. Tooril pursued Jamukha. Temujin pursued the Taichuuds and defeated them at Ulengu Turas. Temujin was wounded in the battle but was saved by Zelme. The Taichuuds were able to disperse. Sorkhon Shar along with his sons Chuluun Baatur and Chimbai joined Temujin. Zev joined Temujin. [14]

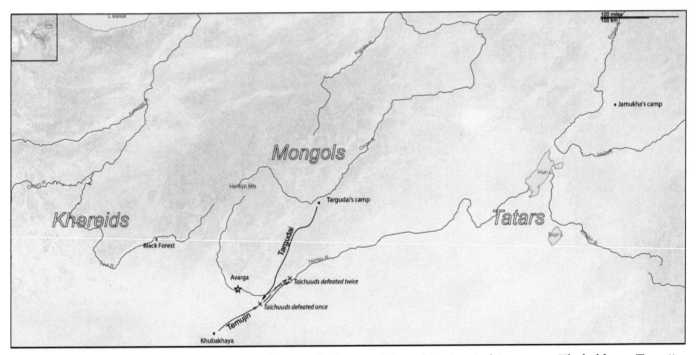

Targudai regrouped the Taichuuds and moved to attack Temujin. Warned in time in his camp at Khubakhaya, Temujin moved at once. He defeated them and Targudai retreated. Temujin then pursued and defeated them again. Targudai was seized by some of his followers but they decided to let him go. Targudai was later killed by Chuluun Baatur. [15]

The following year, Temujin campaigned against the Tatars and crushed them in two battles at Dalan Nermurges and Ulkhu Silugeljed. Temujin took the Tatars Yesugen and Yesui as wives. Tooril campaigned against Togtoa of the Mergids and captured the sons of Togtoa, Khutu and Chuluun. [16]

The Naiman warrior, Khogseu Sabrag, attacked Tooril and defeated Tooril's son, Sengum, near Tooril's camp. Khogseu Sabrag captured many people, and freed Khutu and Chuluun. Tooril appealed to Temujin for help. Temujin sent Boorchi, Borokhul, Chuluun Baatur, and Mukhulai with a force that defeated Khogseu Sabrag and rescued the captives. Tooril was grateful and proclaimed Temujin as his son and elder brother of Sengum. Sengum, however, was resentful. [17]

War with the Khereids, 1203

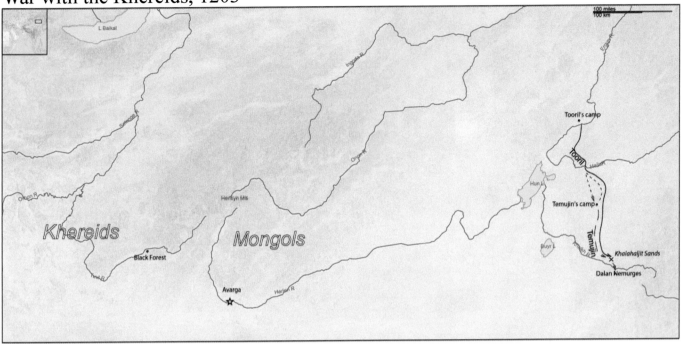

Jamukha and Sengum conspired to convince Tooril to break with Temujin. When Temujin asked Tooril for permission to marry his son, Zuchi, to Tooril's daughter, the request was denied. Then Tooril appeared to change his mind and invited Temujin back as part of a plot to kill him. Temujin traveled towards Tooril's camp but was warned of the plot and returned to his own camp. Tooril, Sengum, and Jamukha then advanced against Temujin and they fought at Khalakhaljid Sands. Sengum was wounded. Temujin retreated to Dalan Nermurges. [18]

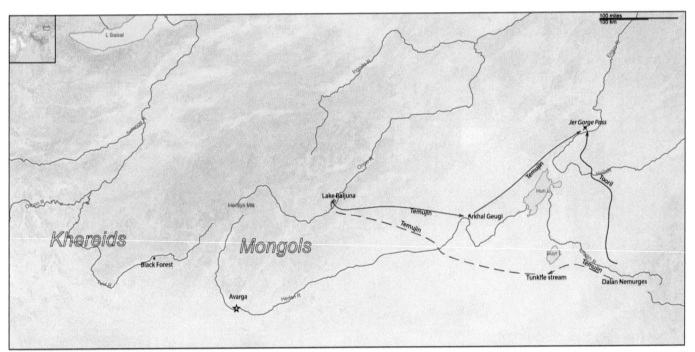

Tooril returned to his camp. Temujin moved west to the Tunkhe Stream and then with only a few followers moved further west to Lake Baljuna. Temujin regrouped and reassembled his forces. He then advanced, surrounded Tooril's camp, and defeated him in a three day battle at Jer Gorge Pass. Tooril fled and was killed in Naiman territory. Sengum fled and was killed in the far west. Jamukha escaped. Temujin absorbed the Khereids into his forces. Temujin took one of Tooril's nieces for a wife and gave another, Sorkhagtani, to his son Tului. [19]

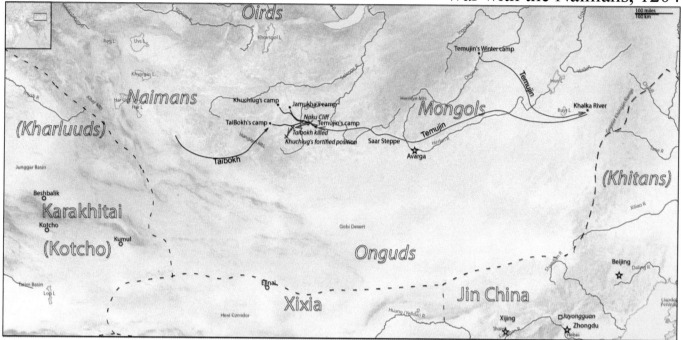

In the spring of 1204, Taibokh of the Naimans, and his son Khuchlug, formed a new coalition against Temujin. Jamukha and the Mergids joined. Taibokh also invited the Onguds to join, but the Onguds did not, and told Temujin of the offer. Temujin moved to the Khalka River to organize his forces, then set out to confront the Naimans. The coalition assembled at Naku Cliff. On May 17, Temujin advanced, surrounded, and defeated them. Taibokh was killed in retreat. Khuchlug tried to fortify a position but could not hold it. He fled west to his uncle, Buirug. The Mergids also fled west. Jamukha fled west, however most of his followers submitted to Temujin. [20]

War with the Mergids, Fall/Winter 1204/1205

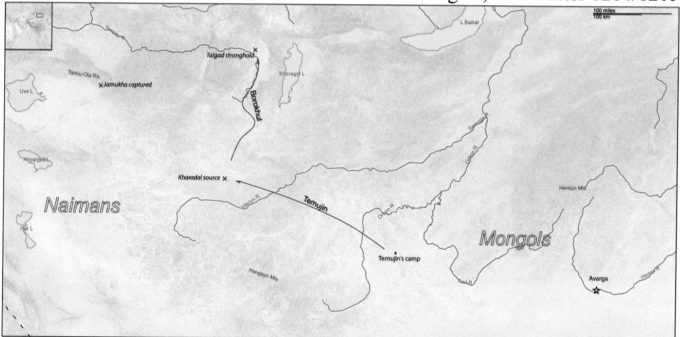

In the fall, Temujin pursued Togtoa to the Kharadal Source and defeated him. Togtoa and his sons Khutu and Chuluun fled west to Buirug. Temujin gave Khutu's wife, Turkhan, to Ogedei. Dayir Usun submitted to Temujin and presented his daughter Khulan to Temujin for a wife. Jamukha was seized by his few remaining followers and turned over to Temujin. Temujin executed them, and then executed Jamukha. In the winter, Dayir Usun revolted. Temujin sent Borokhul, Chuluun Baatur and Chimbai to quell the rebellion. They defeated Dayir Usun at the Taikhal Stronghold. [21]

Raid into Xixia, 1205

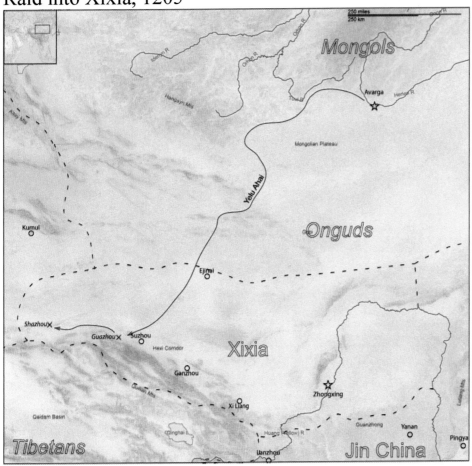

Temujin sent a force under Yelu Ahai to invade Xixia. Bypassing fortified cities, they raided the area of Guazhou and Shazhou. [22]

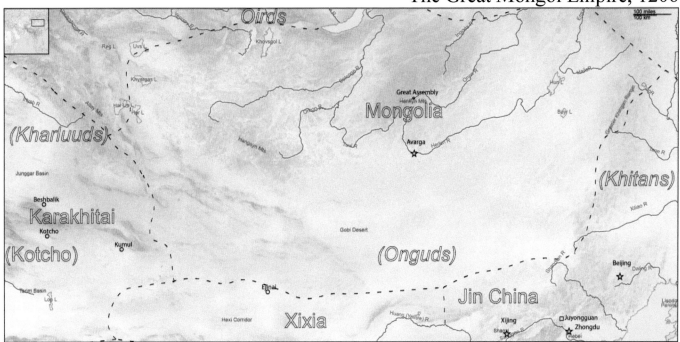

With his enemies destroyed, defeated, or chased to the far west, Temujin called an assembly to proclaim the foundation of the Great Mongol Empire (labeled Mongolia), and proclaimed himself Chinggis Khan. He organized the army and appointed commanders. He formalized an alliance with Alakush of the Onguds. He also rewarded his most loyal followers, Boorchi and Mukhulai, assigned families to his mother, sons, and brothers, and appointed Shikhikhutug as judge. [23]

Chinggis, 1206 to 1227

Countries & Peoples – 1/1/1207

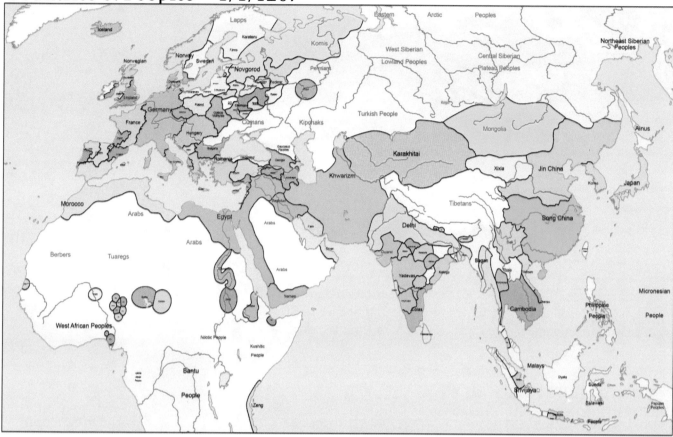

Some principal events between 1160 and 1207.

Africa. New: Walo 1186, Zamfara 1200.

Western Europe. New: Bulgaria from Byzantium 1185, Bohemia from Germany 1198. Morocco took Valencia 1171. Christian coalition-Morocco war 1172-1212. England-France war 1202-1204. Germany-Lombard League war 1167-1183. Germany took Mecklenburg 1167. Germany and Sicily personal union 1167. German civil war 1197-1214. Albigensian Crusade 1208-1229.

Eastern Europe. Fourth Crusade overthrew Byzantium 1204. New from Byzantium 1204: Epirus, Romania, Serbia, Trebizond. Other new: Minsk from Turov 1164, Perieslav/Zaleskii from Vladimir 1175. Halych union with Volyn 1199.

Middle East. Mosul conquered Egypt 1169. Governor of Egypt, Salah ad-Din, usurped control and ruled Egypt 1174. Egypt took Hejaz and Yemen 1174. Egypt took city of Jerusalem 1187. Egypt

dynastic war 1196-1200. Rum took Sivas 1175. New: Ghur from Ghazni 1163. Ghur expanded 1173, defeated Ghazni 1186, defeated by Khwarizm and reestablished in Delhi 1206. New: Khwarizm from Karakhitai 1173. Khwarizm conquered Merv 1193, Hamadan 1194, Kirman 1196, Ghur 1206.

Central Asia. New: Mongolia, wars of unification 1196-1206.

Eastern Asia. Huang (Yellow) River flooded 1194. Civil war in Japan (Gempei war) 1180-1185, Kamakura Shogunate established 1185.

Southern Asia. Calukyas civil war 1156-1189, Yadavas replaced Calukyas. Ghur conquered Sind 1182, Cahamanas 1192, Gahadavalas 1197, Senas 1206. Sultanate of Delhi established 1206.

South-Eastern Asia. New: Kedah from Srivijaya 1160. Srivijaya took Galuh and Sunda 1200. Cambodia-Champa war 1167-1190, 1191-1203.

War with the Naimans and Mergids, 1206

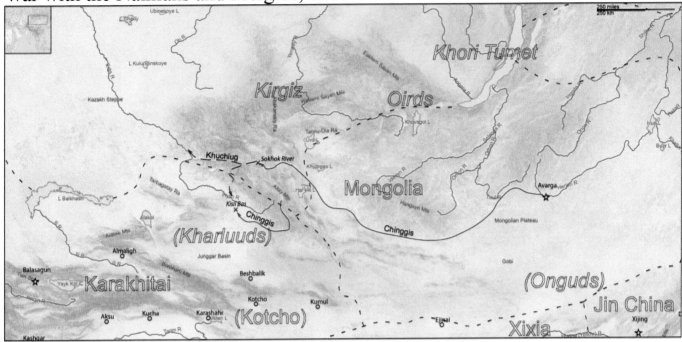

After settling affairs, Chinggis resumed the war against the Naiman and Mergid remnants. He defeated Buirug at the Sokhok River. Khuchlug and Togtoa fled further west to the Irtysh River. Buirug fled across the Altai Mountains. Chinggis crossed the mountains and caught him at Lake Kisil Bas where he was killed. [1]

War with Xixia, 1207/1208

In September, 1207, Chinggis undertook a second invasion of Xixia, this time reaching Wulahai and plundering the surrounding territory. He withdrew in early 1208. [2]

Submission of the Forest People, 1207/1208

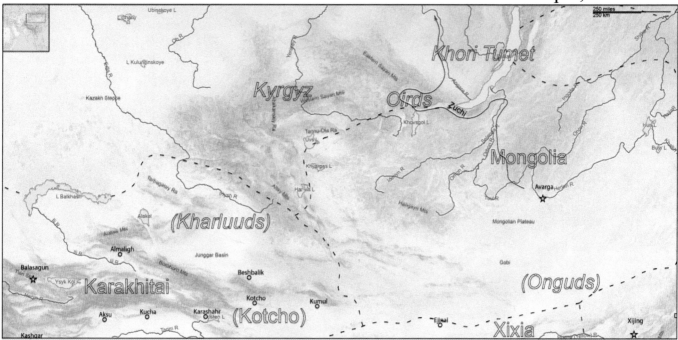

In 1207, Chinggis sent an embassy to the Kyrgyz people which secured their submission. In the fall of 1208, Zuchi led an expedition north into the forests. He secured the submission of the Oirds and other tribes along the Angara River.[3]

War with the Naimans and Mergids, 1208/1209

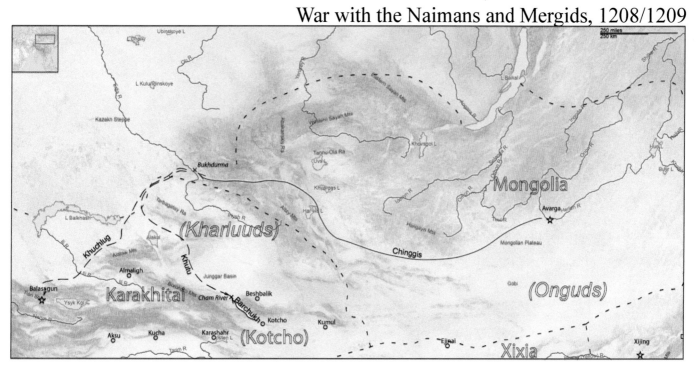

In the fall, Chinggis set out on another expedition against Khuchlug and Togtoa. He found them at Bukhdurma and defeated them once again. Khuchlug fled to Karakhitai where he found refuge. Togtoa was killed and his son Khutu fled to Kotcho. Barchukh, the ruler of Kotcho, denied him refuge and drove him off at the Cham River. Khutu would join Khuchlug in Karakhitai the following year. Later, in 1209, Barchukh transferred his allegiance from Karakhitai to Mongolia.[4]

War with Xixia, 1209

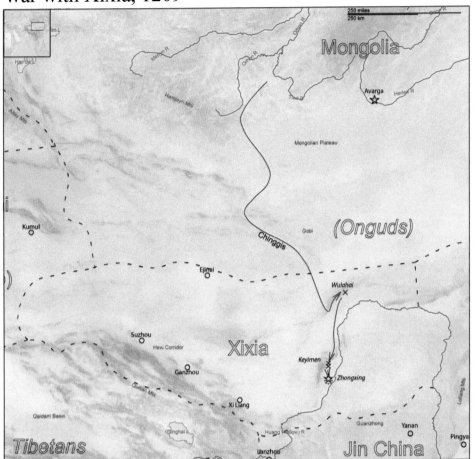

In April, Chinggis began a campaign against Xixia. In May, he defeated a Xixia army at Wulahai and captured that city. Chinggis advanced to Keyimen in June. The initial Mongol advance was defeated but the defenders did not follow up their victory. In August, Chinggis lured the defending Xixia army to defeat. Chinggis then advanced to the Xixia capital, Zhongxing. [5]

Siege of Zhongxing, 1209/1210

In October, Chinggis surrounded the city and made camp by the Royal Tombs to the west. By November, Chinggis had a dike built, to divert waters of the Huang (Yellow) River to the city. In January, the dike broke and the river also flooded the Mongol camp which was then moved to higher ground. As the city remained surrounded, Xixia sued for peace and submitted to Chinggis. Chinggis returned to Mongolia. [6]

In February or March, Chinggis began his invasion of Jin China. He commanded the center column himself. The Three Princes, Zuchi, Tsagadai, and Ogedei, commanded the right wing, and Mukhulai the left wing. Zev and Subeedei led the advance force. They all moved in the spring when conditions for crossing the Gobi were most favorable. With the alliance with the Onguds secured, the Jin border walls posed no obstacle. Chinggis and Mukhulai reached the headwaters of the Luan River, and the Three Princes the bend of the Huang (Yellow) River, in May. There they paused to rest both men and horses.[7]

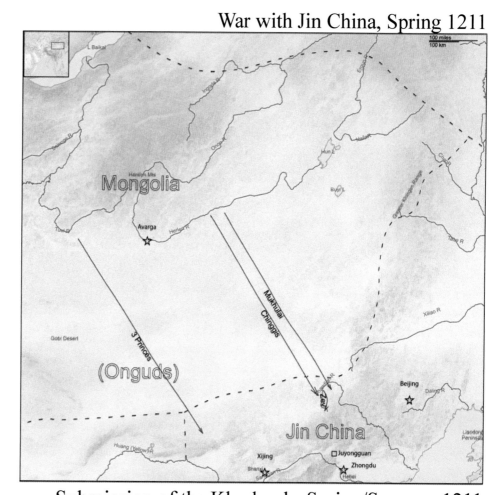

Submission of the Kharluuds, Spring/Summer 1211

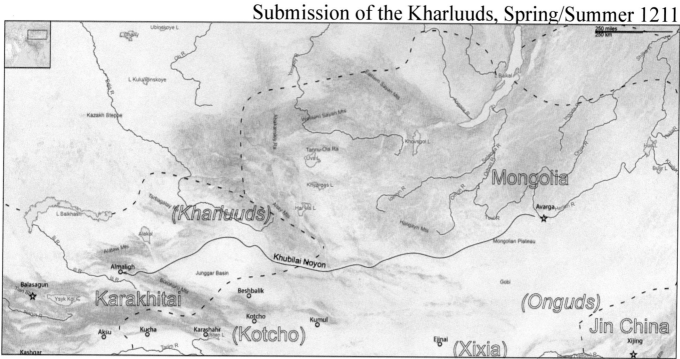

Also in the spring, Khubilai Noyon was sent west towards Karakhitai, where Khuchlug had taken refuge. He secured the submission of the Kharluuds and the city of Almaligh, both of which had been subject to Karakhitai. Shortly after this, Khuchlug deposed the ruler of Karakhitai and took that throne himself.[8]

War with Jin China, Summer 1211

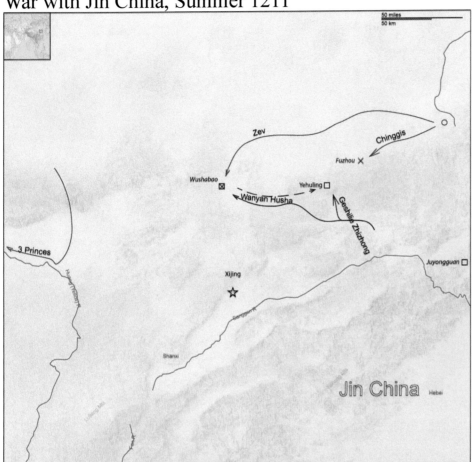

The Jin Emperor sent one army under Wanyan Husha to Wushabao and a larger army under Geshilie Zhizhong to Yehuling. They were to raise fortifications to block further advances by the Mongols. In August, Chinggis sent Zev to attack Wushabao. Zev defeated Wanyan Husha and captured several towns in the area. Wanyan Husha retreated to join Geshilie Zhizhong. Chinggis then advanced to take Fuzhou. The Three Princes, in the meantime, advanced up the Huang (Yellow) River and captured large numbers of horses from the Imperial grazing grounds. [9]

War with Jin China, Fall 1211

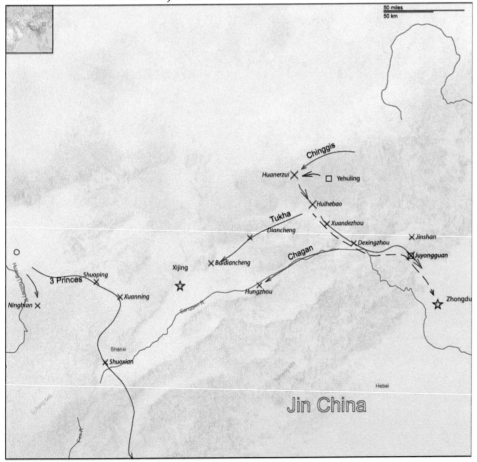

The Mongol and Jin armies met at Huanerzui in October in a decisive victory for the Mongols. Geshilie Zhizhong in retreat was joined by Wanyan Husha. They rallied at Huihebao but were defeated again and fled towards Zhongdu. Chinggis advanced to Xuandezhou and Dexingzhou. Chinggis then sent Zev to probe Juyongguan. Unable to take the pass, Zev lured the defenders into the open, and defeated them. Zev then was able to occupy the pass. Chinggis followed with the main army and camped just north of Zhongdu, After Huanerzui, the Three Princes had led their army towards Xijing, but then turned south, taking several cities along their path. [10]

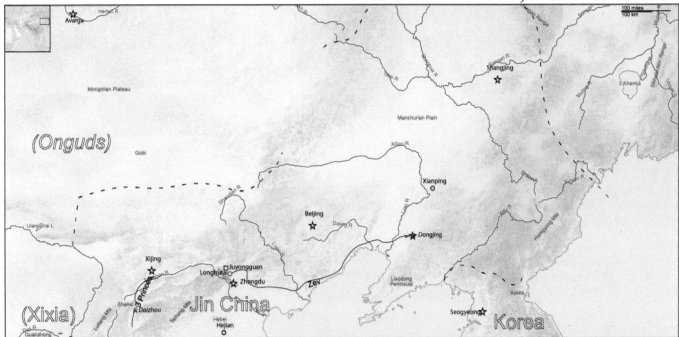

Chinggis made camp at Longhutai in December, and sent out troops to raid the countryside. Zev led a small force to Zhongdu and skirmished with the Imperial Guards. Also in December, the Three Princes turned back north and camped near Xijing, raiding the countryside. In January, Chinggis sent Zev on an expedition to Dongjing in the northeast. Once again Zev was able to lure the defenders out and capture the city by pretending to withdraw. He returned to Longhutai in February. However, being unable to take either Zhongdu or Xijing, Chinggis withdrew all his forces north to the borderlands. All the places captured were reoccupied by Jin troops. [11]

Khitan Revolt and Alliance, Spring 1212

In the spring of 1212, while Chinggis camped in the borderlands, Yelu Liuge, a descendent of the previous Liao Dynasty, led a rebellion of the Khitans against Jin China. Hearing of this, Chinggis sent Shikhikhutug to make an alliance with Yelu Liuge. The mission was a success. [12]

War with Jin China, Fall 1212

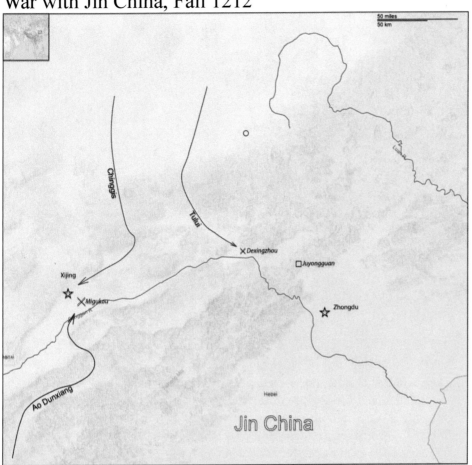

After resting in the grasslands during the summer, Chinggis moved south again in September. He led the main army to Xijing while Tului advanced on Dexingzhou. Ao Dunxiang advanced from the south with a relief army. Raising the siege of Xijing to meet this army, Chinggis won a tremendous victory once again. Resuming the siege, Chinggis was wounded directing an assault and retired. Tului had been unable to take Dexingzhou by this time, but was ordered to make one last attempt which met with success. Both Mongol armies withdrew once again to the borderlands. [13]

War with Jin China, Summer/Fall 1213

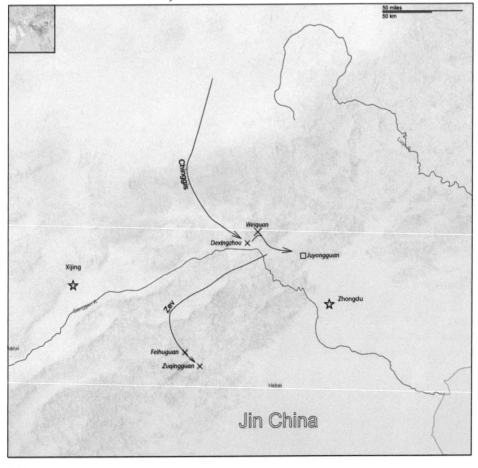

In late summer the following year, Chinggis led his army south and attacked Dexingzhou again. He engaged a large Jin army at Weiquan and destroyed it. The fortifications at Juyongguan had been strengthened and the Mongols were not able to make any headway. In October, Chinggis sent Zev to try and force one of the other passes through the mountains. Zev took Feihuguan and Zijingguan by surprise and secured a passage. [14]

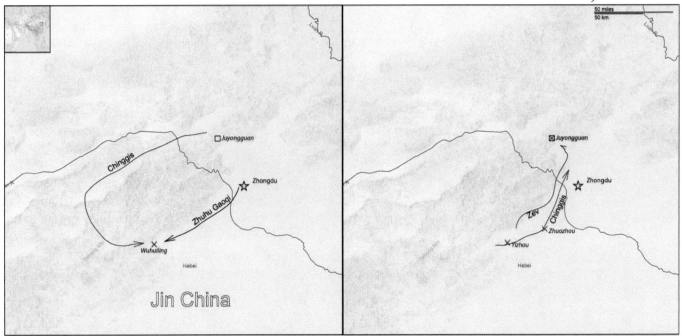

Leaving a small force north of Juyongguan, Chinggis moved the main army to join Zev. Zhuhu Gaoqi moved with a Jin army to block the Mongols but they destroyed him at Wuhuiling. Chinggis then moved on to take Yizhou, and from there sent Zev and Subeedei to attack Juyongguan from the south. Chinggis moved on to Zhuozhou, arriving there on November 10. When Zev had captured Juyongguan, Chinggis left Mukhulai at Zhuozhou and moved back to Longhutai to set up camp. At the end of November, Zhuozhou fell and Mukhulai rejoined Chinggis. Chinggis then surrounded Zhongdu and blocked all roads into the city. [15]

War with Jin China, Winter 1213/1214

With no Jin armies left in the field to oppose him, Chinggis set in motion a sweeping invasion of Jin China by three armies, taking cities and raiding as they went. One was commanded by the Three Princes moving south and southwest. Khasar and the second army stayed close to Zhongdu and concentrated east of the city. The third army, under Chinggis himself. moved south and southeast. Mukhulai and Tului split off parts of this force to widen its area of operation. Not all cities in their paths were captured. Of the Jin provincial capitals, Hejian, Yidu, Pingyang, and Taiyuan fell but Zhending, Daming and Dongping resisted. The Mongol armies did not occupy any of the territory. [16]

First Siege of Zhongdu, Spring 1214

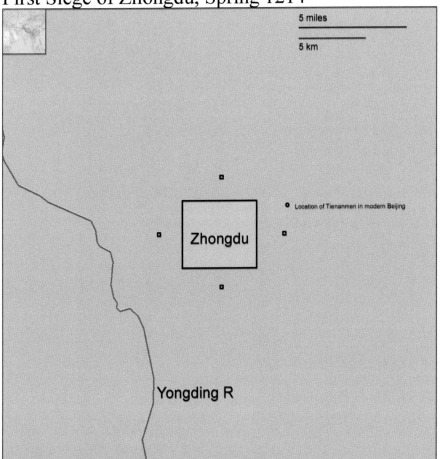

By March, Chinggis, Mukhulai, and Khasar had returned to the vicinity of Zhongdu. The walls of the city were 40 feet high. There were 12 or 13 gates and 900 towers. Outside the walls was a triple line of moats. In addition, there were four fortresses outside the city connected by tunnels. The Mongols first attacked one of the southern gates and penetrated into the city before they were cut off and driven back out with heavy losses. Next a general assault was ordered but the attackers were attacked in the rear by troops from the four fortresses and forced to retreat. In April, negotiations for peace began and the Jin Emperor, Xuancong, agreed to terms in May. A huge tribute was paid, including an Imperial Princess, and Chinggis withdrew, but not very far. By this time the Mongols had set up administration in some of the closer areas. [17]

Flight of the Jin Emperor, Summer 1214

Within a short time of the peace agreement, Xuancong decided to leave Zhongdu for the relative safety of the southern capital, Nanjing. Chinggis took this as a breaking of the peace agreement and prepared to resume the war. [18]

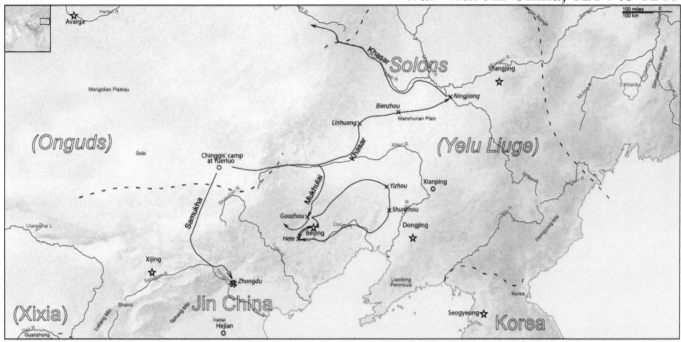

From his camp at Yuerluo, Chinggis sent Samukha with an army in September to invest Zhongdu. Chinggis also sent Khasar and Mukhulai, into the northeast in October to gain control of the Jin homeland. Khasar went north, taking several places and securing the submission of the Solons. He then returned to Mongolia in late winter. Mukhulai turned south towards Beijing, the Jin northern capital. After sending out raiding parties, he made a wide swing to the east to cut off support. Turning back he was met by Jin forces at Hete in February. Mukhulai defeated this army and advanced to Beijing. [19]

Second Siege of Zhongdu, 1214 to 1215

By late September, the Mongols had surrounded Zhongdu again, blocked all roads, and surrounded nearby towns. No assaults were planned, the Mongols were content to wait for the city to fall. Chinggis came to Longhutai himself in January. Shimo Mingan replaced Samukha in April and Chinggis returned to his northern camp. As conditions worsened in the city, one of the two commanders committed suicide and the other one fled, escaping through the Mongol blockade. The remaining officers surrendered to Shimo Mingan in June, and the city was sacked. Chinggis appointed Shikhikhutug to take charge of the booty and administration of the area. Among the captives was Yelu Chucai who Chinggis took into his service. Zhongdu was renamed Yan. [20]

War with Jin China, Spring 1215

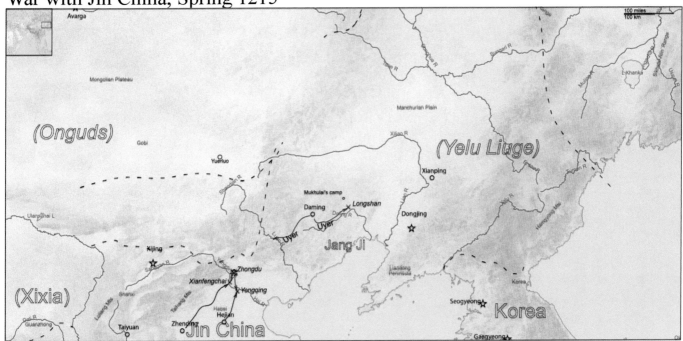

In the northeast, Mukhulai had left Shimo Yexian at Beijing. In early March, Shimo Yexian was able to trick the commander into opening the gates. Mukhulai then sent Uyer and Shimo Yexian out to mop up local forces. The Jin officer sent to defeat Yelu Liuge, Puxian Wannu, rebelled and declared himself independent. Only a foothold remained in Jin control. Two armies had been sent to the relief of Zhongdu in April bringing convoys of supplies. One advanced from Zhending, one from Hejian, Both were intercepted by the Mongols. The Red Coat rebellion broke out in Shandong. [21]

Peace Offer, Summer 1215

After the fall of Zhongdu in June, the Mongols suspended operations in Jin China. This and the loss of the northeast, left Jin China with less than half of its former territory. But what remained was still the most populous and richest part, particularly south of the Huang (Yellow) River. In August, Chinggis sent a peace offer to Nanjing. If the Emperor would cede territory north of the Huang River and become only King of Henan, subject to the Mongols, there could be peace. Xuancong still felt strong enough to refuse. [22]

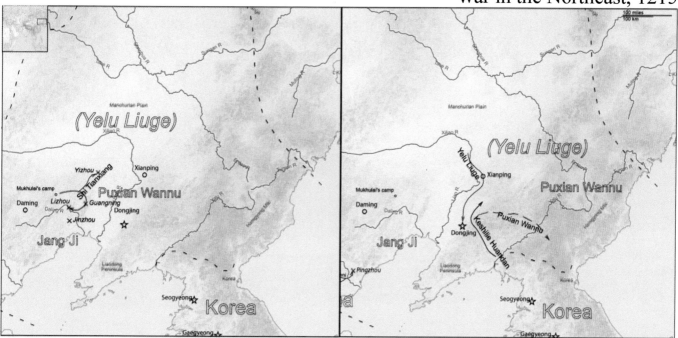

In the summer, Jang Ji rebelled at Jinzhou and soon was in control of the coast between the Daliong and Luan rivers. Mukhulai sent Shi Tianxiang against him in July, but did not attack Jinzhou directly. In September, Shi Tianni recovered Pingzhou (see below). In October, the Jin commander, Geshilie Huanduan, drove Puxian Wannu out of Dongjing. Puxian Wannu retreated towards Korea. Geshilie Huanduan was recalled, however, allowing Yelu Liuge to move in. Yelu Liuge soon controlled the whole area. [23]

War with Jin China, Fall/Winter 1215/1216

Chinggis had returned to his base in Mongolia in the summer, but had set in motion another sweeping move into Jin territory to the south, to start in September. One army under Tolun Cherbi moved to Zhending. A second army under Shi Tianni moved east to recover Pingzhou from Jang Ji, and then joined the first army at Zhending. A third army moved west to Xijing and then south into Shanxi. A fourth army was planned under Samukha, but he was waiting for reinforcements from Xixia. By February, the first three armies had returned to the north. [24]

War in the Northeast, 1216

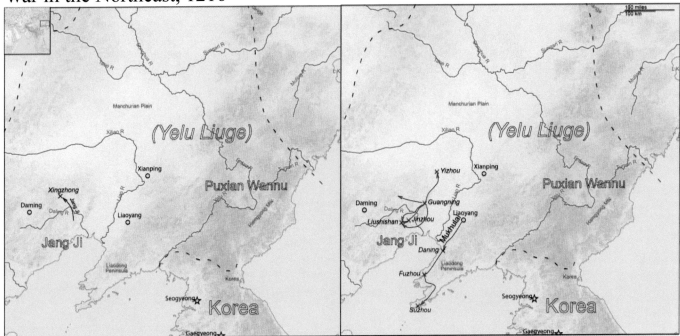

Jang Ji went on the offensive and attacked Xingzhong. Mukhulai waited until summer to respond. He sent Uyer to attack Liushishan and when Jang Ji sent a force to meet Uyer, Mukhulai moved with his full force and Jang Ji's force was destroyed. Mukhulai then laid siege to Jinzhou. It surrendered in September. Mukhulai then recovered Xinzhong and defeated rebels in Guangning and Yizhou. In October, Mukhulai campaigned against some Khitan rebels in the Liaodong peninsula with support from Yelu Liuge. Seeing this, Puxian Wannu submitted in November. Mukhulai then returned to Mongolia to meet with Chinggis and plan future operations against Jin China. [25]

War With Jin China, Fall/Winter 1216/1217

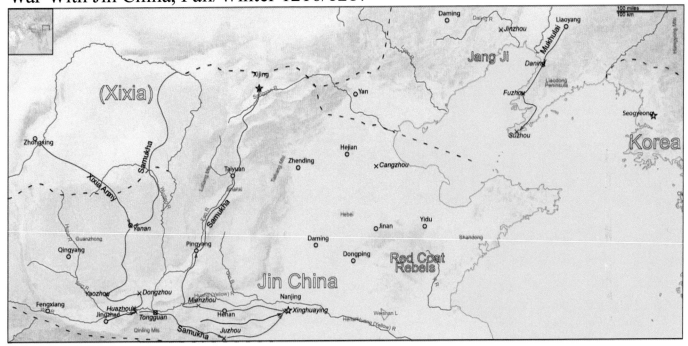

By September, the Xixia troops were ready to move and Samukha crossed the Huang (Yellow) River. The two forces met at Yanan and continued south. After crossing the Wei River, Samukha was met by a Jin army from Jingzhao which he defeated. Moving west he captured the Tongguan fortress. More Jin armies were mobilized to block his possible path east. Turning south he was pursued by one of these. The armies met near Nanjing and Samukha was forced to turn back. Defeating another army at Mienzhou, he crossed the Huang River again and moved north to Pingyang. There the Xixia contingent left to return home. Samukha moved on to Xijing in February which surrendered. [26]

War with the Mergids, 1216/1217

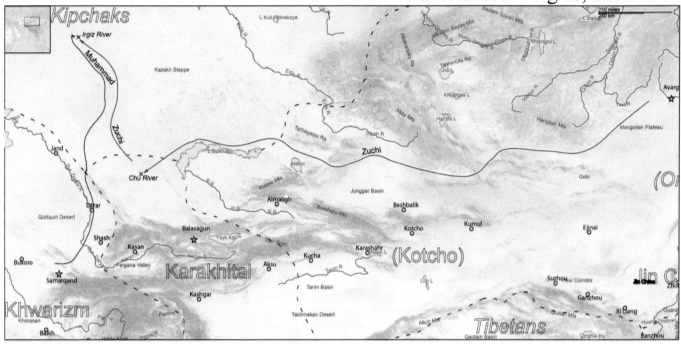

Khutu had quarreled with Khuchlug at Balasaghun and led his remaining followers north to the area along the Chu River. Zuchi and Subeedei were sent to put an end to them. At the same time, Muhammad, ruler of Khwarizm, undertook a campaign against the Kipchaks. Zuchi defeated Khutu on the Chu River, pursued him further north, and defeated him again. Khutu was captured and Chinggis would order his execution. The Khwarizm army came upon the scene after the battle and clashed with the Mongols. This battle was indecisive. [27]

Revolt of the Forest People, 1217   # War in Korea, 1218

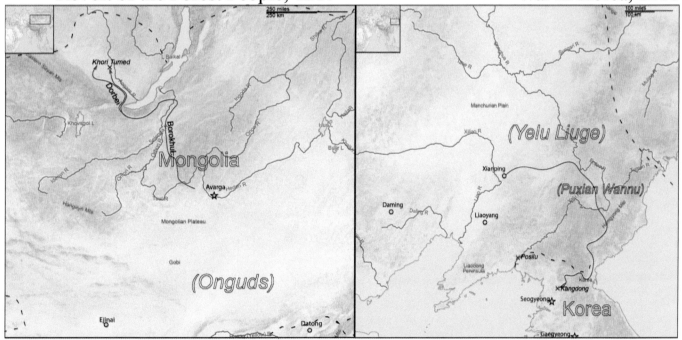

In 1217, the Khorii Tumed people revolted and captured their Mongol representative. Another, sent to negotiate his release, was also captured. Borokhul was then sent with an army to secure their release but he was ambushed and killed. Dorbei was then sent with another army which finally brought them under control. [28]

There were still Khitan rebels holding out at Kangdong in Northern Korea. Yelu Liuge sent a force against them in January. With support from Puxian Wannu and Korea, they surrounded the town, which surrendered in March. At the end of the campaign, Korea submitted to the Mongols. [29]

War with Jin China, Fall/Winter 1217/1218

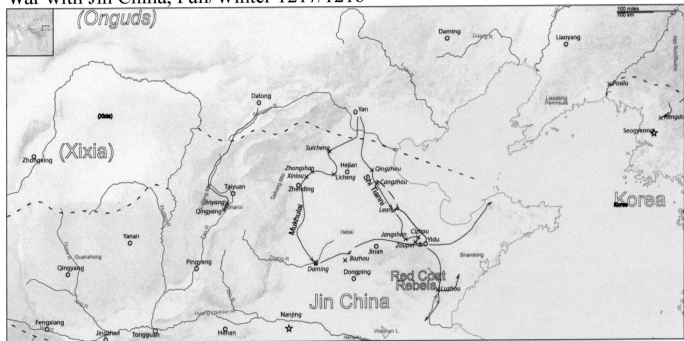

Mukhulai was now in command in China. Leading the center army himself, Mukhulai moved south in September. He reached Daming and captured it in December. At the same time, Shi Tianni advanced with the left wing. The Jin commander at Cangzhou retreated and was met by reinforcements from Yidu. They gave battle at Lean but were defeated. Shi Tianni continued and captured Yidu in January, supported by additional troops from Mukhulai's force. The right wing raided Shanxi as a diversion. [30]

War with Khuchlug, 1218

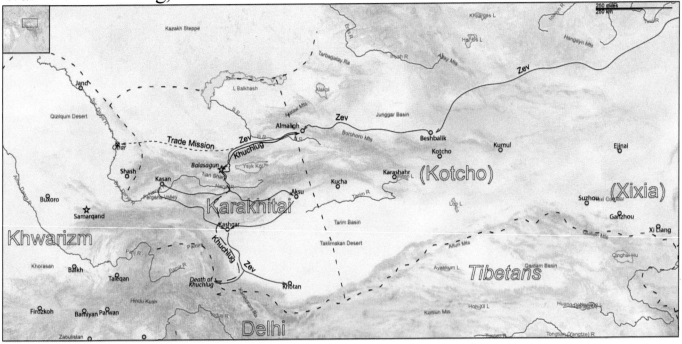

In 1218, Khuchlug attacked Almaligh. Zev was sent to destroy him once and for all and started out in the summer. Khuchlug retreated from Almaligh as the Mongols approached. Zev defeated Khuchlug outside Balasaghun and occupied the city. Khuchlug fled south with Zev in pursuit. Zev also sent a detachment to Kasan where the local governor, Ismail, submitted peaceably. As Zev continued, Ismail tracked Khuchlug down and killed him. Zev would remain in the west. Perhaps following on Zev's campaign, a Mongol trade mission to Khwarizm arrived at Otrar. The governor of that city, claiming that they were spies, seized their goods and executed them all. [31]

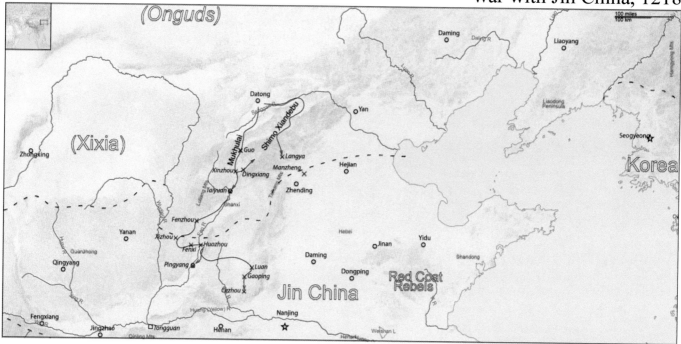

In March, Jin forces reoccupied most of the area the Mongols had moved through. Mukhulai moved south in the fall, taking towns in Shanxi. An army under Shimo Xiandepu moved towards Zhending. He was met at Langya where he defeated a Jin force. The Jin commander, Zhang Ruo, was captured and then defected with all his troops. Zhang Ruo was then sent to confront Wu Xian, the Jin commander at Zhending, and defeated him at Manzheng. [32]

Revolt of the Forest People, 1218/1219

The Kyrgyz had been asked to support the suppression of the rebels of 1217, but they had refused and revolted themselves. Other Forest People also joined in. Zuchi was sent to restore order in the forest. He subdued the Kyrgyz and moved on deep into Siberia before returning in the spring of 1219. [33]

War with Jin China, 1219

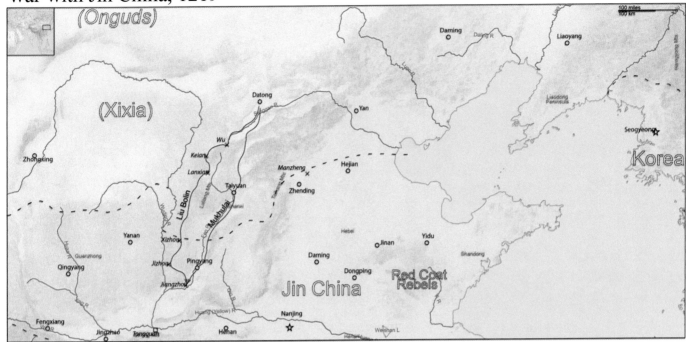

In 1219, Mukhulai made another move into Shanxi. He led one army down the Fen River valley, securing what he had gained the previous year. A second army under Liu Bolin and Shi Tianxiang moved on a parallel route to the west, capturing more towns. Both armies met at Jiangzhou. Meanwhile, Zhang Ruo and Wu Xian fought several more battles at Manzheng, with Zhang Ruo eventually capturing Wu Xian's forward position. [34]

Chinggis Moves West, 1219

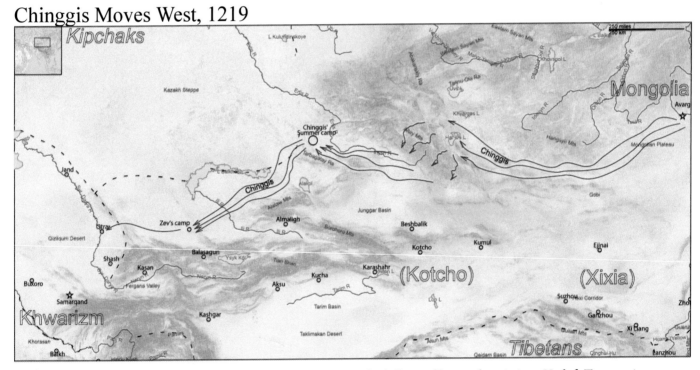

Chinggis began moving west with his army in May, to avenge the killing of his trade mission. He left Temuge in command in the homeland, Yelu Liuge in the northeast, and Mukhulai in China. By June, the army had reached the foothills of the Altai Mountains and prepared to cross. They probably spread out to use all the available passes and came back together on the Irtysh River. There the army rested until October before moving on. The columns recombined and met up with Zev's force on the Chu River. They all moved towards Otrar in November. [35]

After arriving at Otrar, Chinggis put Tsagadai and Ogedei in charge of the siege. He sent Zuchi north, to subdue towns along the Syr Darya River. He sent Zev south along the river with a small force to Banakat. He took the main army himself with Tului, bypassed the capital at Samarqand, and advanced on Buxoro. Most of the garrison attempted to break out three days after the Mongols arrived but were defeated in battle. The city then surrendered but a few held out in the citadel for another twelve days and the city was sacked. Muhammad, the ruler of Khwarizm, fled from Samarqand even before the fall of Buxoro. Otrar also fell in February and was devastated in punishment for the killing of the trade mission. [36]

War with Khwarizm, Winter 1219/1220

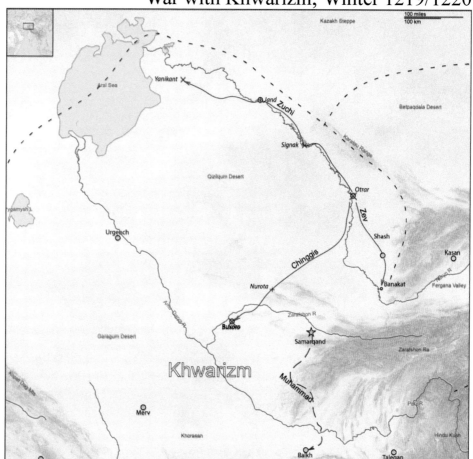

War with Khwarizm, Spring 1220

Chinggis and Tului then advanced on Samarqand from the west. Tsagadai, Ogedei, and Zev converged from the east. The Mongols attempted an assault and when the garrison counterattacked he drew them off with a false retreat, slaughtering most of them. The city surrendered on March 12 and was sacked, but the citadel held out until late April. [37]

War with Khwarizm, Spring/Summer 1220

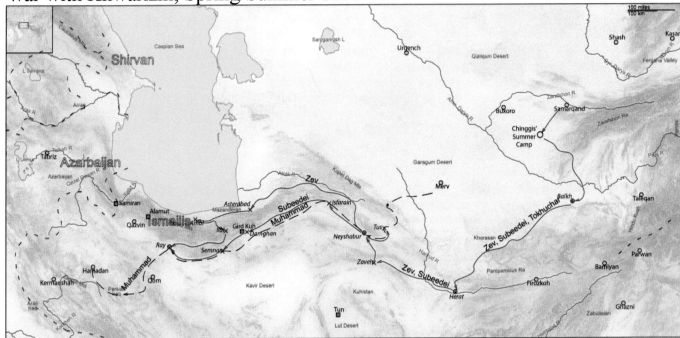

After the fall of Samarqand, Chinggis camped to the south for the summer. In May, Chinggis ordered Zev and Subee-dei to hunt Muhammad down. He had moved on to Neyshabur by then. Zev and Subeedei moved quickly, passing on from cities that surrendered and taking those that did not. They almost overtook Muhammad at Neyshabur. They then split up and met again at Ray by the end of summer. Muhammad had moved on to Hamadan in the meantime. [38]

War with Jin China, Fall/Winter 1220/1221

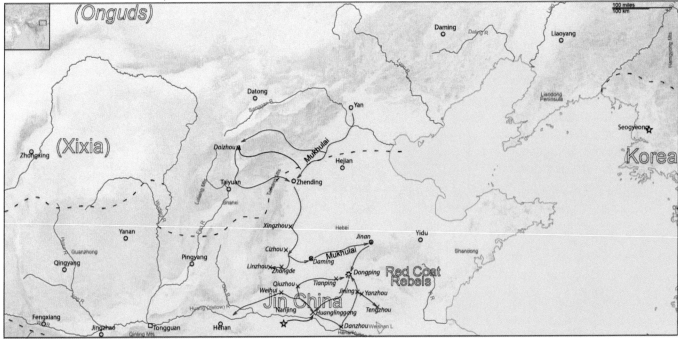

Mukhulai moved south again in September, advancing on Zhending. A detachment defeated a Jin diversion at Dai-zhou. Wu Xian surrendered Zhending in October, and joined the Mongols. Mukhulai continued south taking Zhangde, and Daming by November. He then took Jinan and turned back to Dongping. A new Jin army was assembled at Huanglinggang, forcing Mukhulai to move against it. Victorious, he sent detachments east and west, then went back to Dongping. After unsuccessful assaults, he set up a blockade of the city and returned north. [39]

Chinggis directed Zuchi to move south to take Urgench, the original capital of Khwarizm. Zuchi moved in October. His advance force took Khiva and once the main army arrived they began a siege of Urgench. When the city did not fall quickly, Chinggis sent Tsagadai with reinforcements. When Tsagadai arrived, the two princes quarreled. Chinggis finally sent Ogedei to be in charge, but Urgench still did not surrender. Later in the fall, Chinggis himself moved to Tirmid and crossed the Amu Darya River in January. [40]

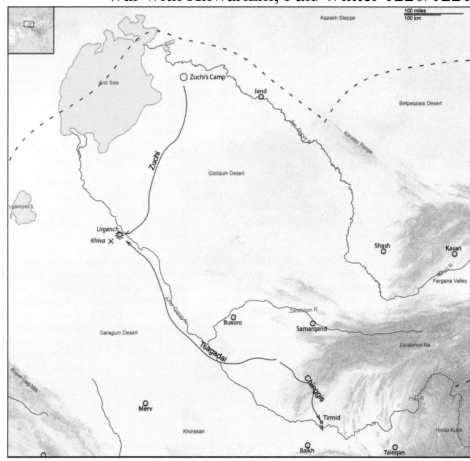

Zev and Subeedei continued their pursuit of Muhammad. Muhammad had left Hamadan moving towards Baghdad but soon turned back. Then he barely escaped at Hamadan, where a new army that he had assembled was defeated and the city surrendered. The Mongols continued pursuit as he fled to the shores of the Caspian Sea. However, they could not catch him before he sailed off to an island. He died on the island in December. [41]

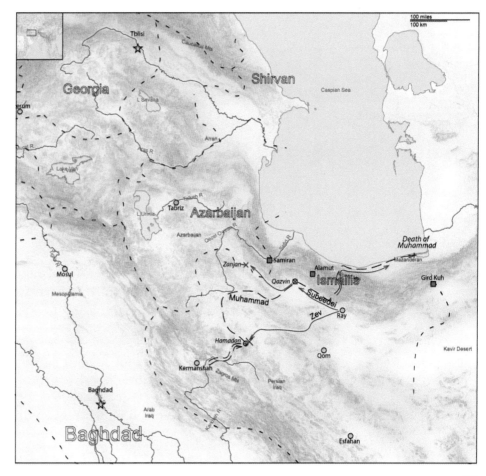

Western Expedition, Winter/Spring 1221

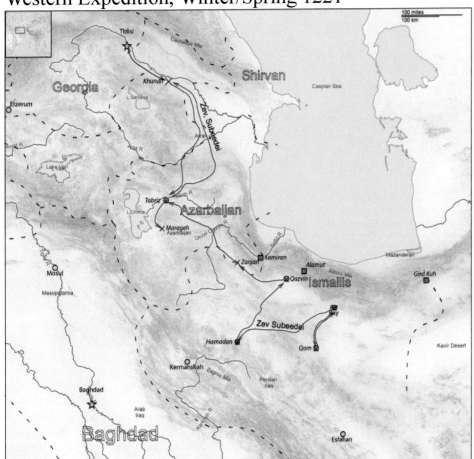

Following the death of Muhammad, Subeedei reported to Chinggis and received orders to remain with Zev in the west. They proceeded to move through the area, sacking Ray and Qom in February. Hamadan surrendered and they moved on to take Qazvin and Zanjan. Next Tabriz surrendered and from there, they moved to Georgia where they defeated a Georgian army at Khunan. By March they were back in Tabriz. From there they took Marageh. [42]

War with Khwarizm, Spring/Summer 1221

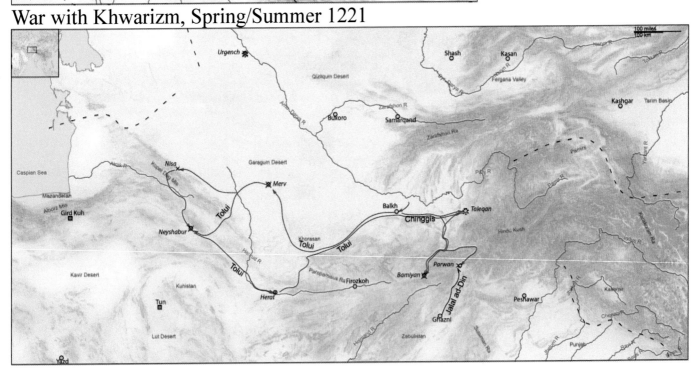

In the spring, Chinggis advanced to take Balkh and then split his forces. Tului was sent west, while Chinggis split his forces further to move south. Chinggis himself advanced to Taleqan while he sent probes to Bamiyan and Parwan. Tului had to fight to take Merv and Neyshabur and both were devastated by April. Herat surrendered and was spared. Urgench fell in April as well. Chinggis next marched on Bamiyan where his favorite grandson, Mutegen, had been killed in fighting. Bamiyan was devastated. Muhammad's son, Jalal ad-Din, had been gathering forces at Ghazni and took an opportunity to advance on Parwan, where he defeated Shikhikhutug. [43]

War with Khwarizm, Fall 1221

Several cities had revolted after Parwan, including Balkh, Merv, and Herat. Chinggis, however, first moved with his full force to avenge the defeat. Jalal ad-Din retreated to India. Chinggis followed, bypassing Ghazni, and defeated Jalal ad-Din's army on the banks of the Indus River in September. Jalal ad-Din himself escaped across the river. [44]

Western Expedition, Fall/Winter 1221

Moving south in August, Zev and Subeedei went to Hamadan again, which resisted this time and had to be taken. Back at Tabriz, they moved on to Georgia, taking several towns, and defeating the Georgians a second time at Bardev in November. They were at Derbent by the end of the year. [45]

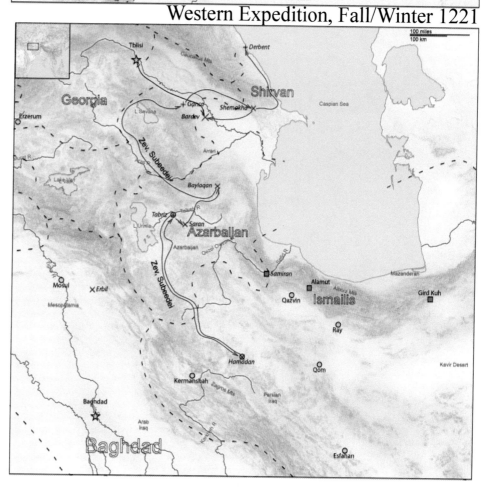

War in Persia, 1222/1223

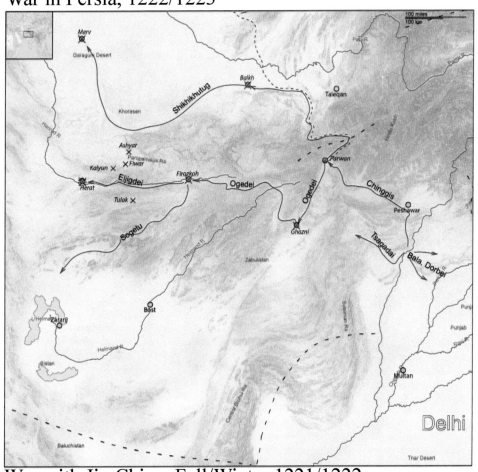

Chinggis now turned his attention to wiping out the resistance that had developed after Parwan. He himself moved back to Parwan. Shikhikhutug was sent to recover Balkh and Merv, and Ogedei went to Ghazni and Firoz Kuh. Eljigedei moved on to Herat, and other detachments were sent into Sistan. All were successful, even though the siege of Herat lasted eight months. Chinggis sent Bala and Dorbei east across the river, in pursuit of Jalal ad-Din. Chinggis also sent Tsagadai to search west of the river, having heard that Jalal ad-Din had come back to bury his dead. Other smaller places were taken as well. Chinggis moved back to the north by the end of the year. [46]

War with Jin China, Fall/Winter 1221/1222

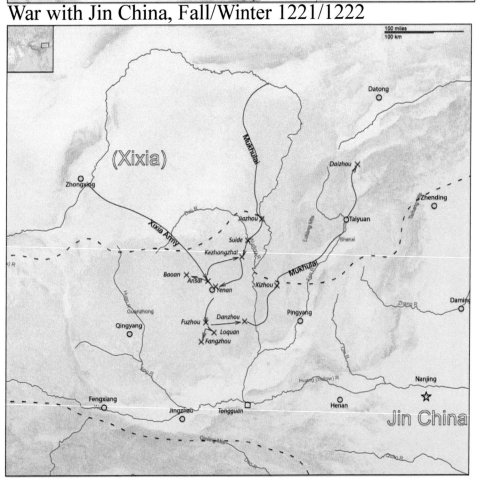

Mukhulai advanced into Guanzhong in October and took Jiazhou without opposition. A Xixia army came to support the invasion but was defeated at Ansai on its own and joined Mukhulai at Kezhongzhai. The combined army then moved on Yenan and defeated Wanyan Heda's army but could not take the city. Mukhulai continued south. After he received news that Xizhou had been lost and Daizhou had revolted, he had to turn back in March to deal with this problem. [47]

Western Expedition, 1222

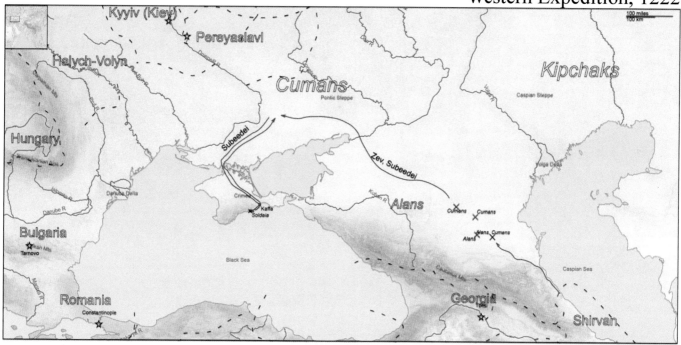

After passing the Caucasus Mountains at Derbent, Zev and Subeedei came out on the Caspian Steppe. There they were confronted by a coalition of tribes: Alans, Circassians, and Cumans. After an initial inconclusive battle, the Mongols defeated each of them separately. They then moved north, and Subeedei continued into Crimea. There he made contact with the Venetians at Kaffa and sacked the Genoese trading post of Soldaia. After this, he rejoined Zev on the Pontic Steppe. [48]

War with Jin China, Fall/Winter 1222/1223

Mukhulai set out again in August, moving down the Fen River Valley and pacifying Shanxi once again. Shi Tianxiang moved on a parallel route to the west. They advanced to Hezhong and built a bridge over the Huang (Yellow) River. When the bridge was completed in December, Mukhulai moved into Guanzhong. Finding Jingzhao too strong, Mukhulai detached Monkhbokh to move on Fengxiang directly while he reduced other towns himself. Another Xixia army was called upon to help besiege Fengxiang. [49]

Western Expedition, 1223

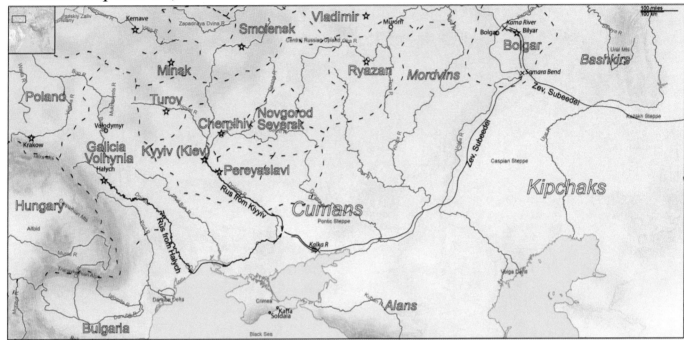

The Cumans and several Rus principalities got a force together to confront the Mongols. Zev and Subeedei retreated eastward in May, leading the coalition into the steppe. After eight days, the Mongols turned and won a decisive victory at the Kalka River. They then turned north and moved towards Bolgar. The Bolgar ruler, Ilgram, ambushed the Mongol advance force at Samara Bend, but Zev and Subeedei came up with the main army and defeated him near the Kama River. Zev and Subeedei then returned east to rejoin with Chinggis. Zev died along this final part of the expedition. [50]

Conflict with Song China 1223

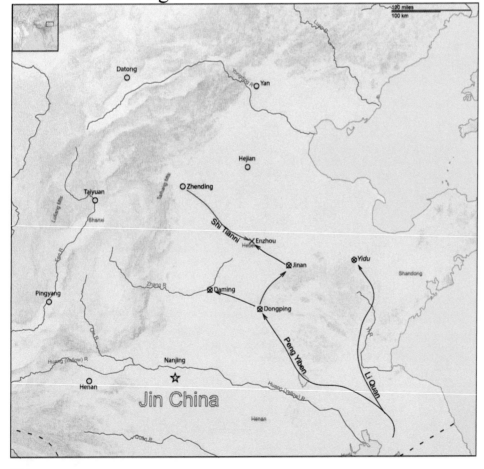

In the fall of 1222, Song generals Peng Yiben and Li Quan invaded Hebei and Shandong, capturing Yidu in January and Dongping in April. In the summer, Peng Yiben advanced further but was turned back by Shi Tianni at Enzhou. [51]

Defection of Xixia, 1223-1224

Xixia had provided armies to support Mukhulai in his campaigns against Jin China. However, in 1222, under a new emperor, and with Chinggis still in the far west, Xixia withdrew its army and its allegiance. With no support, Mukhulai was forced to retreat from Guanzhong in March 1223 and he died in April at Wenxi. Xixia then sought an alliance with Jin China. A punitive expedition under Shi Tianxiang marched against Xixia in the fall but withdrew when threatened by a Jin force in the rear. Mukhulai's son, Bol, led another expedition in the fall of 1224 and captured Yinzhou. [52]

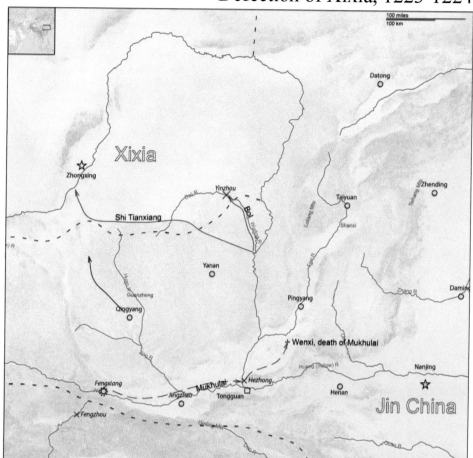

Chinggis Returns, Fall 1223 to Spring 1225

Chinggis spent part of the winter near Samarqand. In January 1223, he crossed the Syr Darya River and moved on to Shash. He spent the summer of 1223 north of Shash. Subeedei returned from his western expedition in the fall, but Zuchi remained at his camp north of the Aral Sea. By summer 1224, Chinggis was at the earlier campground on the Irtysh River. Crossing the Altai Mountains at the end of summer, he returned to Mongolia in February 1225. Chinggis' return journey was more in the way of a triumphal procession than a military campaign. There were frequent stops for hunting and feasting. [53]

Invasion of India, 1224

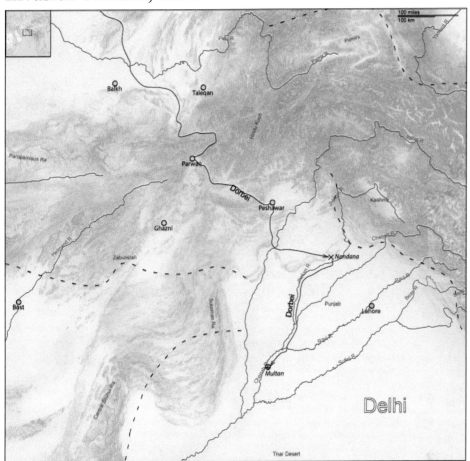

Before Chinggis left the west, he had ordered Dorbei back to India to search for Jalal ad Din. Dorbei crossed the Indus River early in 1224 and captured Nandana. He then moved south to Multan and besieged it for 42 days. However, by this time Jalal ad-Din had already left India and was in Western Persia. The hot weather caused Dorbei to abandon the siege in April. [54]

Conflict with Song China, 1224/1225

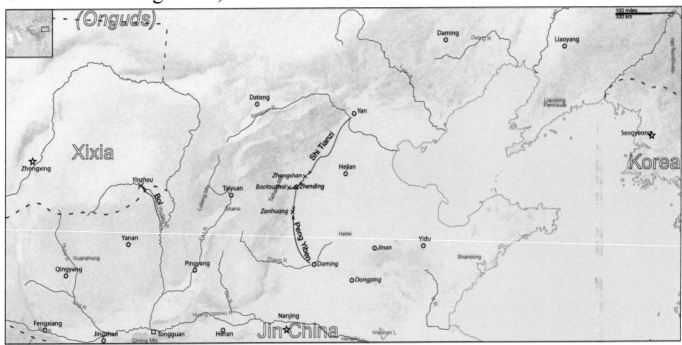

In March 1224, Wu Xian rebelled and killed Shi Tianni, giving Zhending to Song China. Shi Tianni's brother, Shi Tianzi, escaped to Yan. He returned to defeat Wu Xian at Zhongshan in April, and reoccupied Zhending. The following year in July, Shi Tianzi defeated and killed Peng Yiben at Zanhuang. Wu Xian fled to Baotouzhai and was defeated again. He finally fled to Nanjing. [55]

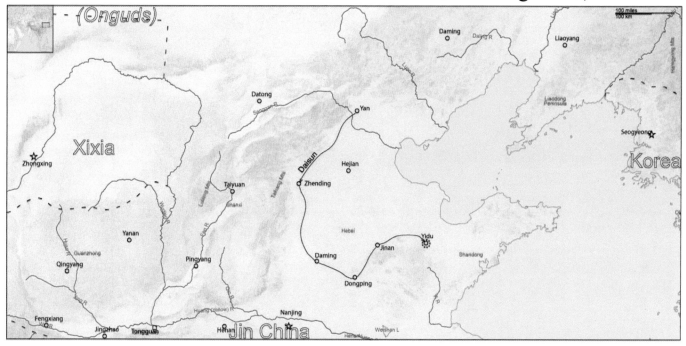

In the fall of 1225, Mukhulai's brother, Daisun, moved south retaking the territory Song forces had occupied. A final episode occurred in April 1226 when Li Quan retook Yidu. Daisun besieged the city from October 1226 until May 1227, when Li Quan surrendered and was confirmed as governor of the province under the Mongols. [56]

War with Xixia, 1225/1226

In late 1225, Chinggis moved south against Xixia. He paused to make a winter camp where he was injured during a hunt. Chinggis moved south again in the spring and paused for the summer. At the same time, Subeedei advanced from the west, taking the cities of Xixia one by one, except for Xiliang which surrendered. Bol approached from the east. Chinggis moved south again in November and laid siege to Lingzhou. A Xixia army came out to meet him and he easily defeated it just east of Ling-zhou. He then settled in for a siege of the Xixia capital. [57]

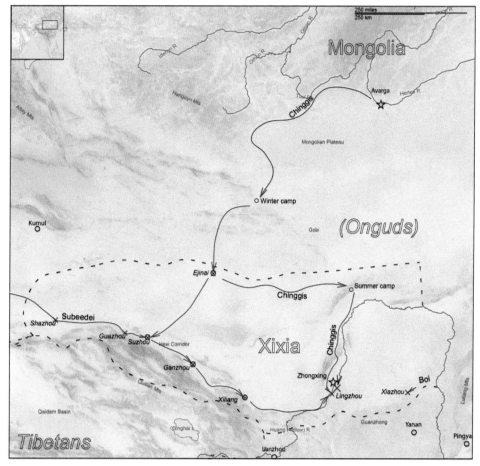

55

War with Xixia, 1227

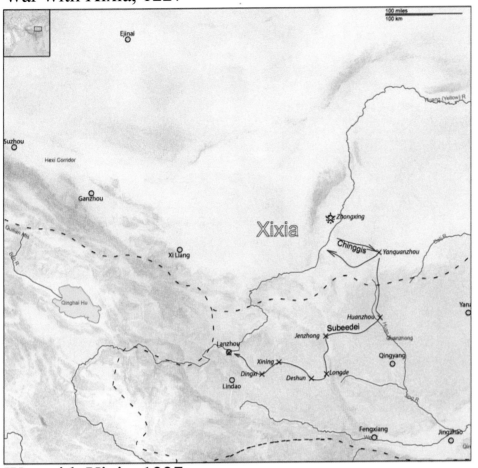

Chinggis sent Subeedei south into Jin territory. Subeedei moved against Jin cities in the upper river valleys. When he could not capture them immediately he left blockading forces. Chinggis in the meantime reduced more Xixia cities while waiting for Zhongxing to fall. [58]

War with Xixia, 1227

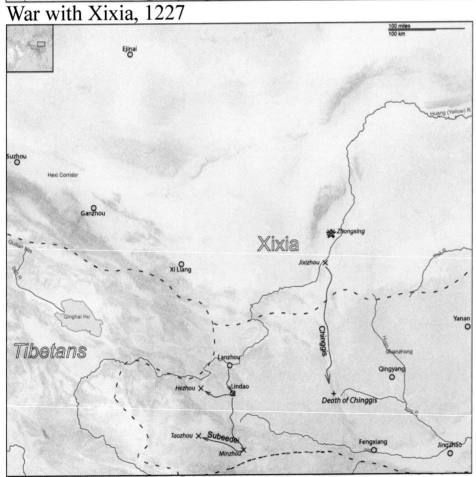

While Subeedei continued to move up the rivers, Chinggis moved south to complete the capture of Longde which Subeedei had only blockaded. While there, he fell ill and moved up into the cooler mountains. He died there in August 1227. His body was carried back to Mongolia and buried in secret. Zhongxing surrendered shortly afterwards and was sacked and devastated. [59]

War in Persia, 1227

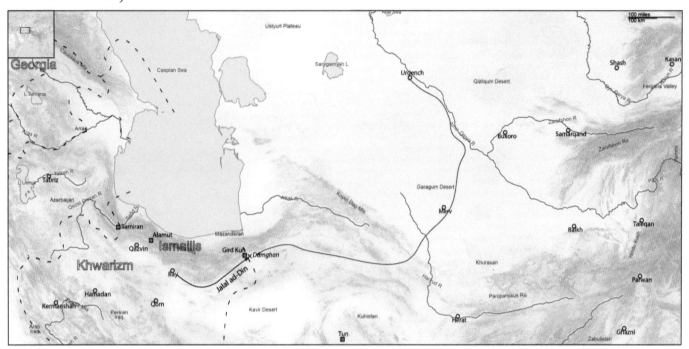

Since returning from India in 1223, Jalal ad-Din had been able to reconstitute a Khwarizm domain in Western Persia. The Mongol commander in Urgench sent a force against him in 1227. Jalal ad-Din, who was campaigning against the Ismailis at the time, attacked and defeated this force at Damghan. [60]

Countries & Peoples – 1/1/1228

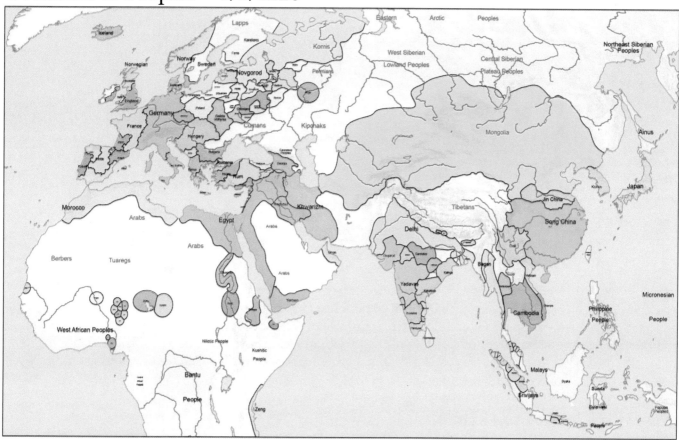

Some principal events between 1207 and 1228.

Africa. No significant events.

Western Europe. Christian coalition-Morocco war 1172-1212. German civil war 1197-1214. Albigensian crusade 1208-1229. England-France war 1213-1216.

Eastern Europe. New: Nicea 1208. Romania-Byzantine war 1208-1222. Mongol western expedition 1222-1223.

Middle East. Mongolia-Khwarizm war 1218-1223. Rump Khwarizm restored 1225.

Central Asia. Mongolia-Xixia war 1209-1210, Xixia submitted 1210, defected 1225, renewed war 1226-1227. Mongolia-Karakhitai war 1216-1217.

Eastern Asia. Mongolia-Jin China war 1211-1215, 1215-1222. Korea submitted to Mongolia 1218, defected 1225.

Southern Asia. New: Kadamba, Pandyas, and Telegucoda from Colas 1216. Candellas took Kalicuris 1211. Hoysalas and Kalacuris took Cola territory 1216.

South-Eastern Asia. New: multiple small countries in Malaya and Sumatra c1200, Singhasari in Java 1222.

Regency of Tului, August 1227 to September 1229

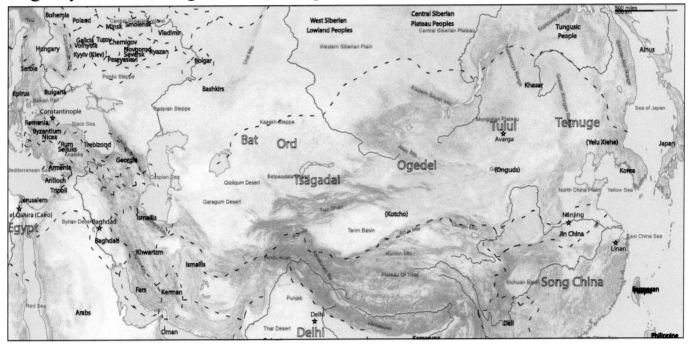

After the death and burial of Chinggis, Tului assumed the Regency in accordance with Mongol tradition as the youngest son. Family members and old faithful allies were confirmed in their territories. The conquered territories in China and Persia were to be administered centrally. Tului's regency continued for two years until a formal assembly met to choose the next Great Khan. Ogedei was selected. Only some minor operations were undertaken during this time. [1]

War with Khwarizm, 1228

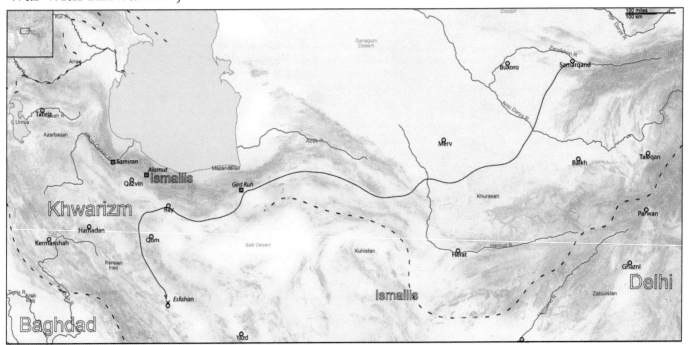

Another Mongol force was sent in the summer of 1228 to deal with Jalal ad-Din. The armies met at Esfahan in August. Both sides suffered heavy losses, and both claimed victory. However, the Mongols retreated to Ray and Jalal ad-Din continued to build up his domain. [2]

Chuluun Baatur attacked Qingyang in 1228 but was defeated by Wanyan Yi at Daqang. Ogedei sent Dogolkhu against Tongguan early in 1230 but Subeedei was unable to support him from the west, Dogolkhu was defeated by Wanyan Heda and forced to retreat. [3]

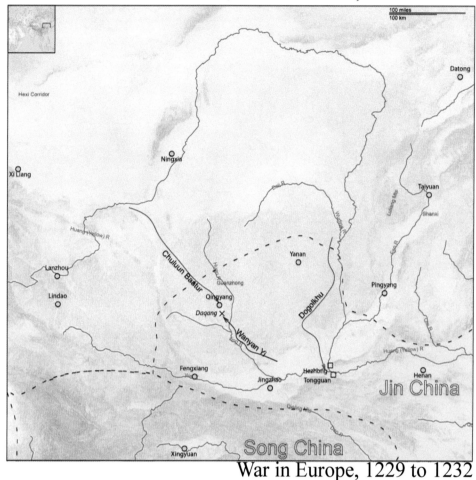

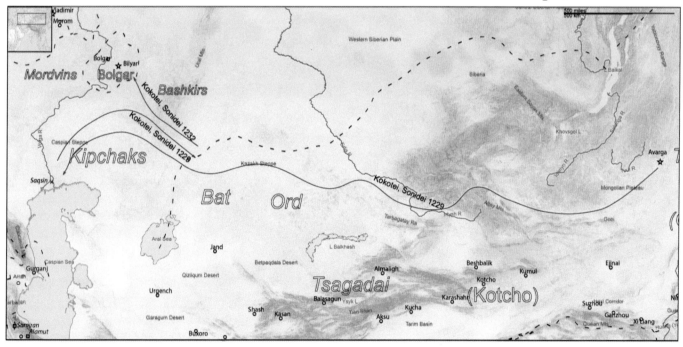

Zev and Subeedei had only passed through Kipchak territory in 1223. In 1229, Kokotei and Sonidei were sent west to bring all the Kipchaks under Mongol rule. They first attacked the Kipchak town of Saqsin. Many of the Kipchaks submitted, others fled north to Bolgar, but others, under Bachman, would continue to resist. The Mongols then defeated Bolgar forces along the Ural River. Bolgar made peace with the Rus princes to avoid having to fight on two fronts. In 1232, the Mongols resumed the offensive, attacking some of the eastern towns of Bolgar, but they could not advance further. [4]

Chormagan Moves West, 1230

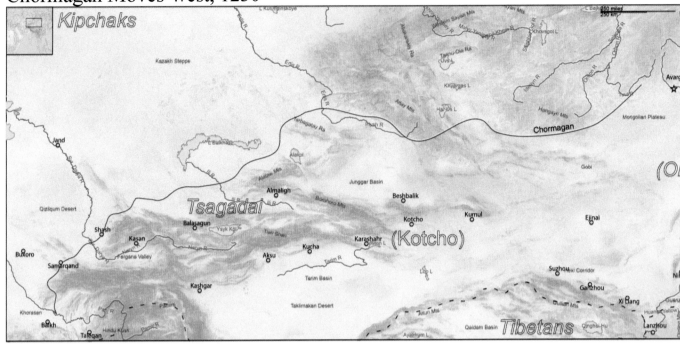

In 1230, Chormagan was sent with a sizeable force to Persia. He probably followed the same path Chinggis had used in 1219. Setting out in the spring, he arrived on the Amu Darya River in the fall and prepared to move on.[5]

War with Jin China, 1230/1231

In the fall of 1230, Ogedei moved south from Datong for a final assault on Jin China. Wu Xian defeated Tas near Luzhou but had to retreat when defeated by Eljigedei. Wanyan Heda rescued Wu Xian but lost Weizhou. Ogedei crossed the Huang (Yellow) River and moved against cities in Guanzhong. Subeedei led the advance force across the Qinling mountains but was defeated by Wanyan Yi in the Daohui valley. The Mongols then turned west to besiege Fengxiang. Yila Pua led a relief force from Tongguan but had to retreat. Wanyan Heda and Yila Pua then attacked Mongols at Huazhou but were defeated. Fengxiang fell in May 1231. Jin forces withdrew from Jingzhao and the remaining cities in the area surrendered.[6]

War with Khwarizm, Fall/Winter 1230/1231

Chormagan left part of his force in eastern Persia with Dayir and moved west to Ray where he established a base by the end of 1230. From Ray he sent a force after Jalal ad Din who had been fighting in the west. Jalal ad-Din fled at their approach and they turned back without finding him. [7]

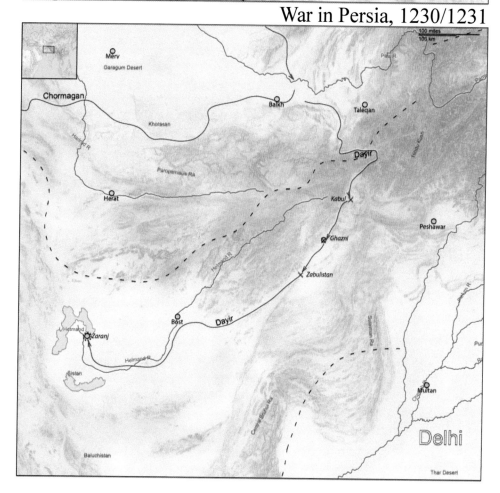

War in Persia, 1230/1231

Dayir was charged with re-establishing Mongol control in eastern Persia. First, he retook Kabul and Ghazni, then continued south to Zabulistan. From there he went on to Sistan where he laid siege to Zaranj. [8]

War with Khwarizm, 1231

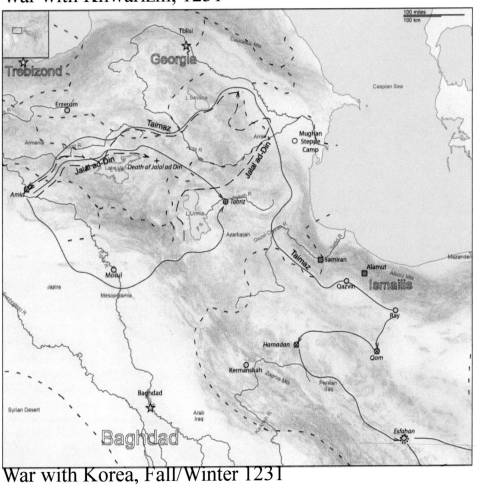

Chormagan sent a force under Taimaz to chase down Jalal ad-Din. Jalal ad-Din fled from place to place and narrowly escaped from a battle at Amid. Finally, fleeing without followers, he was killed by bandits in the mountains. At the end of the campaign, The Mongols occupied Tabriz which did not resist. While Chormagan stayed at Ray, his main force advanced to take Qom and Hamadan. Moving on to Esfahan, it could not be taken quickly so the Mongols left a blockading force. Detachments also went to Shiraz and Kirman in southern Persia and the rulers of those provinces submitted without resistance. [9]

War with Korea, Fall/Winter 1231

Korea had resumed its independence from the Mongols in 1225. In August 1231, Sartai led a Mongol army across the Yalu River. Several towns in the north quickly surrendered. Guju, however, held out under siege. Korea mustered an army at Anbukbu but was defeated. Seogyeong, the western capital, was bypassed. By November, Sartai was at Gaegyeong, the central capital. Korea sent envoys to negotiate a surrender. [10]

Tului had probed Song defenses in the summer. In September, Ogedei advanced from the north with support of forces from Jingzhao and took Hezhong after a thirty-five day siege. He then was ready to march east. Another small force was left facing Tongguan. In October and again in November, Tului sent envoys to Song China asking for passage for his army. When the envoys were executed, Tului crossed into Song territory anyway and took Xingyuan. While there he sent a probe south to the Sichuan region as far as Langzhou. Turning east, he led his army down the Han River valley. [11]

Tului crossed into Jin territory in January. Wanyan Heda moved south to trap the Mongol army at Dengzhou. Tului, however, advanced to Yushan where he won a major victory. Tului then took Dengzhou and continued towards the Jin capital. One final attempt to stop Tului was made by Wanyan Heda at Sanfengshan. Ogedei had crossed the Huang (Yellow) River in late January and sent reinforcements to Tului. During a three-day battle Tului crushed the Jin army. The combined Mongol army reached Nanjing in early February and met up with the the left wing coming from the east. Tongguan was breached and the defenders were caught at Yuling. The city of Henan also fell. [12]

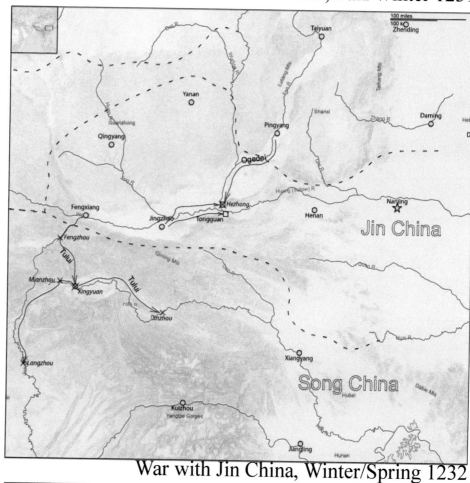

War with Jin China, Fall/Winter 1231

War with Jin China, Winter/Spring 1232

War with Korea, 1232

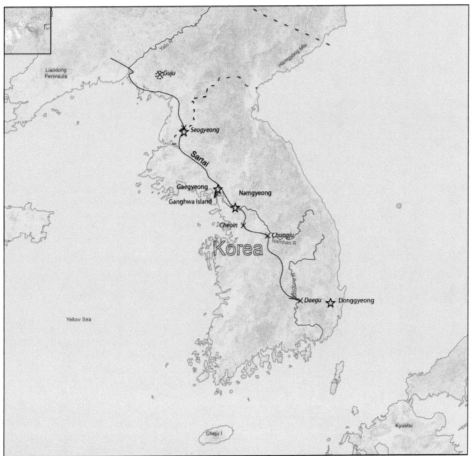

While surrender negotiations with Korea were underway, the Mongols continued the siege of Guju and subdued areas that had been bypassed earlier. Once the surrender had been accepted they lifted the siege of Guju and withdrew, leaving Korean defector Hong Bokwon to govern from Seogyeong. Although Korea had surrendered, they were slow to comply with the terms of surrender. Then in August, under the influence of the Choe family, the Koreans evacuated their capital, Gaegyeong, and moved the entire court to Ganghwa Island. Sartai was quick to respond and came back to the abandoned capital but was unable to cross to Ganghwa Island. He raided further south but was killed at Cheoin and the Mongols withdrew again. [13]

Siege of Nanjing, 1232/1233

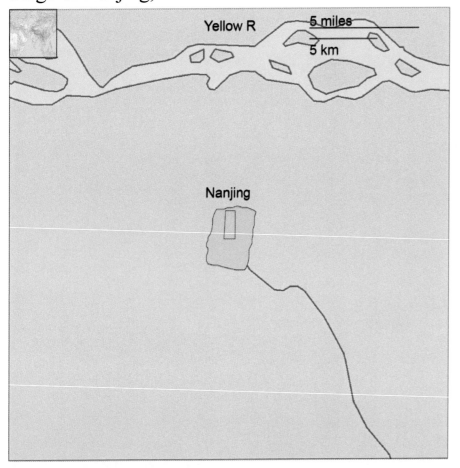

As the Mongol armies converged on Nanjing, Ogedei and Tului returned to Mongolia, leaving Subeedei in charge. The siege began in earnest in April 1232. There was a lull in the fighting during the summer while negotiations were attempted. These failed and the siege continued. One attempt to break the siege was made in August by Jin forces further south but failed. Jin Emperor Aizong fled from the city in February, 1233, and ordered Cui Li to continue the defense. Seeing it was hopeless, Cui Li surrendered the city on February 26. The Mongols changed the name of the city to Bian, the name it had before it was a capital. [14]

Aizong had fled to the city of Guide. In August, he fled from there to Caizhou, further south. He attempted to enlist Song China to come to his defense but instead they allied with the Mongols. Subeedei with the Mongol army, and Meng Gong with a Song army, converged on Caizhou in December. Aizong was unable to escape from this and committed suicide as the city fell on February 9, 1234. As summer approached, the bulk of the Mongol army moved back to the north. [15]

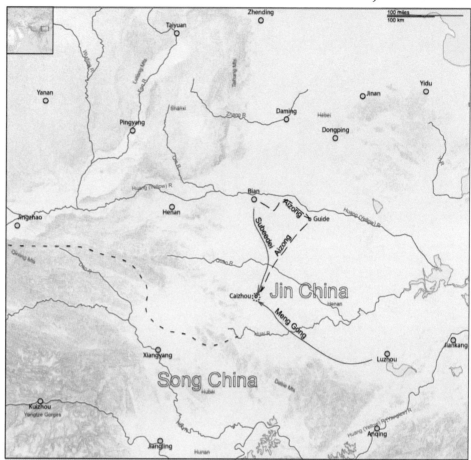

War in the Northeast 1233

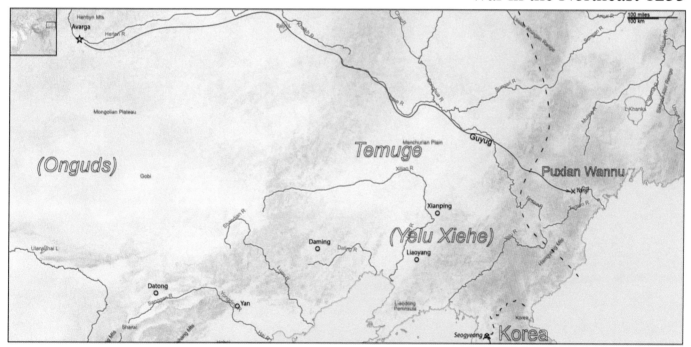

Like Xixia and Korea, Puxian Wannu in the Northeast had also resumed his independence. Guyug was sent from Mongolia to deal with this. Guyug attacked Puxian Wannu's stronghold at Yanji and captured him. [16]

Also in 1233, Korea mounted an offensive which recaptured Seogyeong. Hong Bokwon fled north to safety. This presumably happened some time after Guyug had returned to Mongolia. [16]

Conflict with Song China, 1234

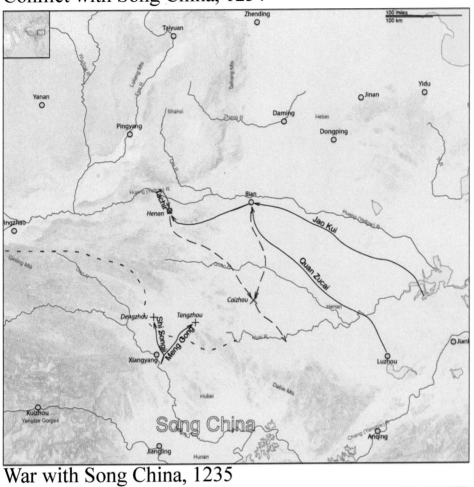

Ogedei had agreed to turn over three districts to Song China for their help in the victory over Jin China. Song forces occupied Caizhou, Dengzhou, and Tangzhou as a result. However, when the main Mongol armies withdrew to the north, the Song government decided to take the former Jin territory for itself. Two Song armies were sent north in the summer to converge at Bian. Part of these forces then moved on to Henan. At this point in the fall, a Mongol army under Tachir crossed the Huang (Yellow) River and defeated them. The Song armies were forced to retreat. They kept the original three districts agreed to however. [17]

War with Song China, 1235

The real war with Song China began in 1235 with probes into Song territory. Khuchu moved to take Tangzhou and went on to raid Caoyang and Yingzhou. The Mongols kept Tangzhou and took Dengzhou as they moved back. Godan led a force to Mianzhou in the west but Song general Cao Yuwen defeated him there. [18]

In 1235, Mongol armies once again invaded Korea to enforce compliance with their surrender terms. In August, Tangut Baatur moved south, retaking the Seogyeong area, and reached Sangju by November. Korea, with the government safely on Ganghwa Island, responded with only local resistance, but many mountain fortresses were able to hold out. [29]

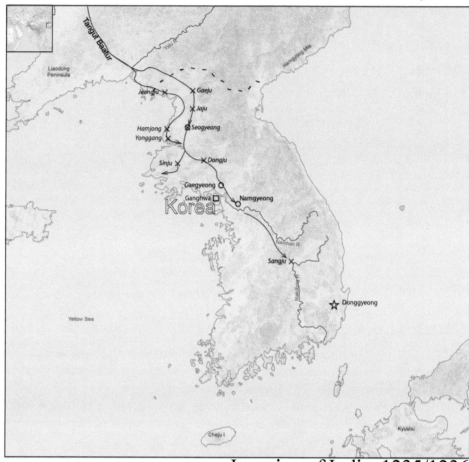

Invasion of India, 1235/1236

The Mongols mounted another invasion of India in 1235 or shortly thereafter. This time Kashmir was taken. [20]

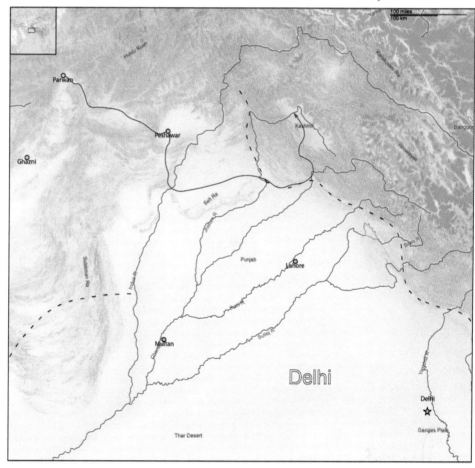

69

Subeedei Moves West. 1235/1236

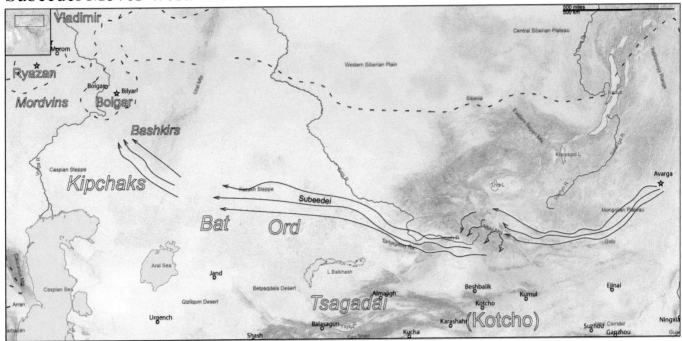

In 1235, Ogedei announced a plan for the next major operation which would be in Europe. The expedition of 1223 had revealed much disunion and weakness there. Bat was appointed in overall command and he left with the advance force in late 1235. Subeedei followed with the main army in the spring of 1236. Many princes from the third generation were included in the army. A significant portion of the army was also made up of Turks and Kipchaks under Mongol command. Subeedei joined up with Bat and the entire army continued to move west. [21]

War in the Middle East, 1235/1236

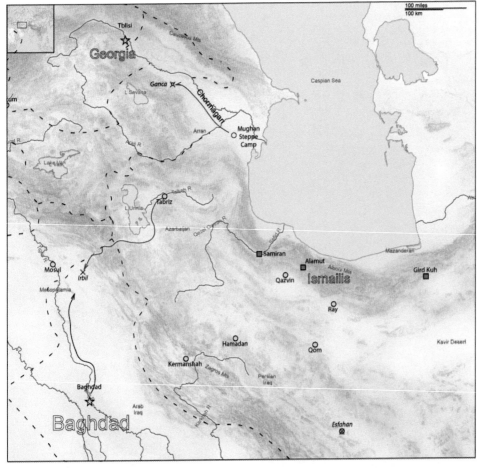

While Bat and Subeedei moved west, Chormagan became active again. In early winter 1235, he advanced on Ganca and took that city, making it a base for future operations. Chormagan also sent a force to Irbil. The city surrendered but the citadel held out. The Mongols withdrew as an army moved towards them from Baghdad. Finally, in 1236 Esfahan was captured after a long blockade. [22]

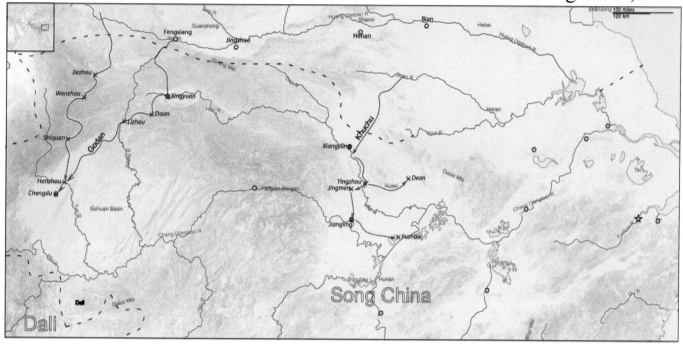

Khuchu moved south early in 1236. Song troops at Xiangyang mutinied, allowing the Mongols to take control. Khuchu moved on to Yingzhou and reached Jiangling on the Chang (Yangtze) River. Godan's main thrust was into the Sichuan region in the summer. He moved south from Fengxiang while a second column worked its way through the mountains to the west. The two columns united before Chengdu. The Mongols took the city but did not hold it. Khuchu died in November, however, and operations ceased. [23]

War with Korea. 1236

Tangut Baatur swept south again in April 1236, penetrating to Goransa Temple by November. The Korean government, however, remained defiant on Ganghwa Island which the Mongols were unable to reach. [24]

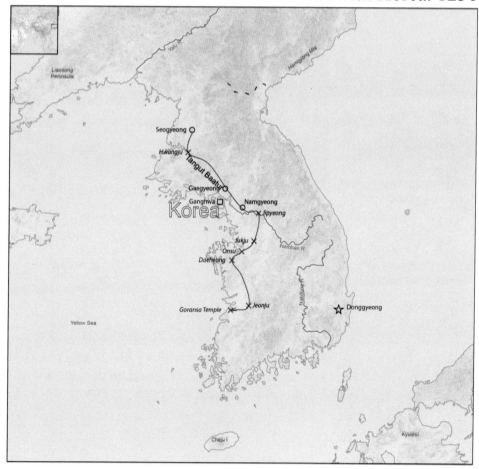

War in Europe, 1236

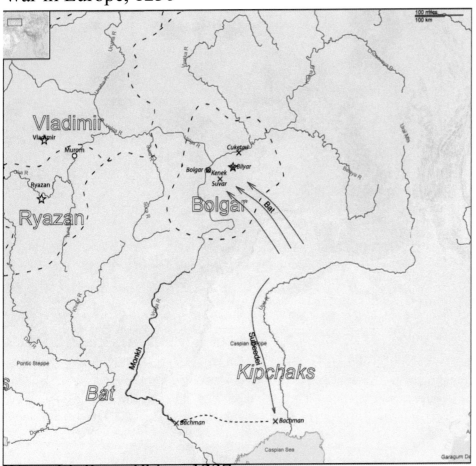

When Subeedei arrived in the west, his first order of business was to subdue the remaining Kipchaks. Using only the advance force, he decisively defeated them on the shores of the Caspian Sea but one of their chiefs, Bachman, was able to flee. Bat, with the entire force, then moved against Bolgar. By the fall, all of the cities of Bolgar had been taken. In the winter, Monkh was sent to search for and destroy Bachman. Monkh moved down the Volga River by boat, with forces following on both banks by land. Bachman was captured and killed on an island where he had taken refuge. [25]

War with Song China, 1237

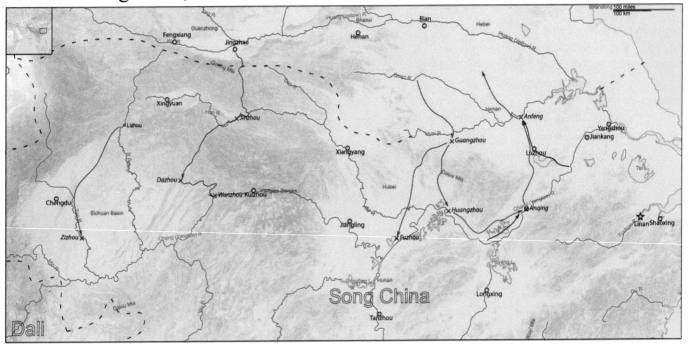

In the fall of 1237, more probes were sent into Song territory. The eastern probe was able to capture Fuzhou but otherwise was unsuccessful. Song counterattacks forced it to retreat. In the west, a force from Jingzhao moved south through the mountains as far as Wanzhou where it remained. The army at Lizhou attacked Zizhou unsuccessfully. [26]

In early winter 1237, Bat crossed the Volga River and moved north along the Don River. When Ryazan and Vladimir refused his demands for submission, the invasion of Rus began. Quickly taking Ryazan on December 21, the Mongols moved along frozen rivers to Vladimir which fell on February 7. Yuri of Vladimir came with a relief army from Yaroslavl but was too late. From Vladimir the army split up. Bat continued east, Subeedei went northwest, and Boroldai pursued Yuri to the north. Yuri was caught and defeated at the Sit River on March 5. The only significant resistance was encountered by Subeedei at Torzhok which was taken after a two-week siege also on March 5. [27]

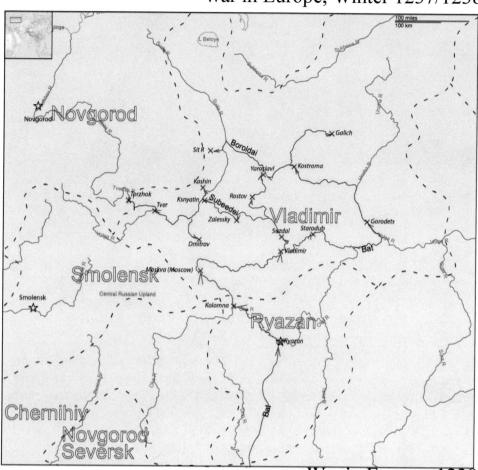

After taking Torzhok, Subeedei continued northwest towards Novgorod. Novgorod was spared by making a promise of submission and Subeedei turned south. Bat and Boroldai also turned south. Subeedei took Vshchiz in the territory of Chernihiv. Bat attacked Kozelsk but was held up by strong resistance. Subeedei joined him there, but Kozelsk still held out for seven weeks before being taken. The Mongols then returned to the Pontic Steppe. [28]

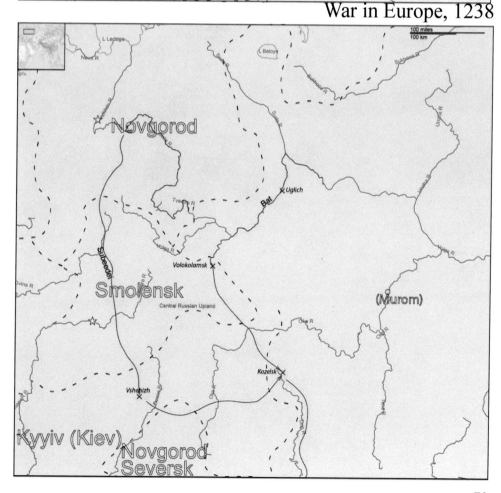

War with Song China, 1238

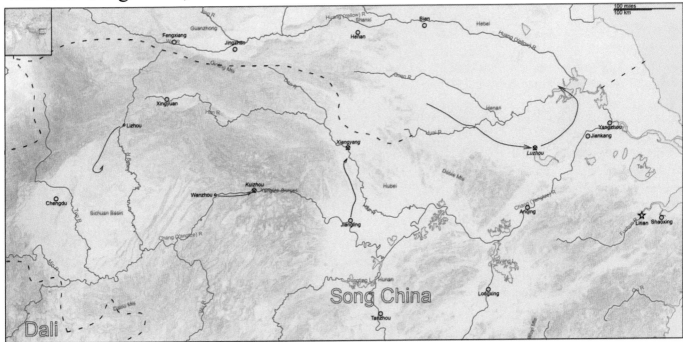

In 1238, the Mongols attempted to negotiate a truce with Song China. By the summer these negotiations had come to nothing and a Song army was able to recover Xiangyang. Later in the year a Mongol army moved against Luzhou. The force from Wanzhou moved on against Kuizhou. The force from Lizhou also moved south again but soon turned back. All the Mongol efforts were unsuccessful. [29]

War with Korea, 1238

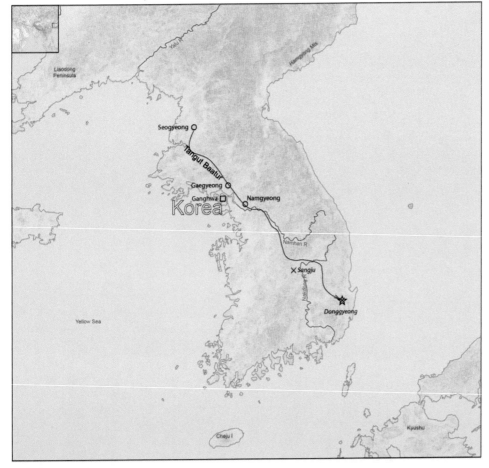

Tangut Baatur moved south again, this time reaching the eastern capital, Donggyeong. Finally, Korea agreed to submit, send the crown prince to Mongolia, and remove the government from Ganghwa Island. [30]

From his base at Ganca, Chormagan sent columns out across Georgia. Many mountain fortresses were taken. Queen Rusudan fled west as the Mongols approached Tblisi. [31]

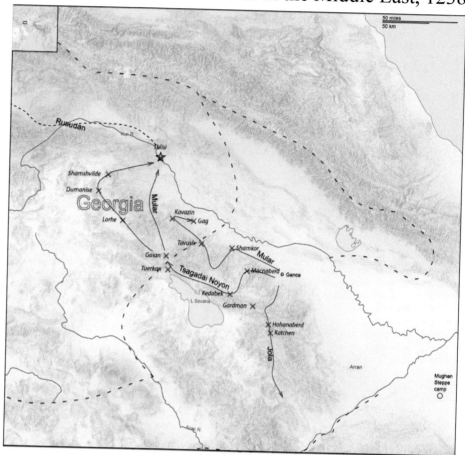

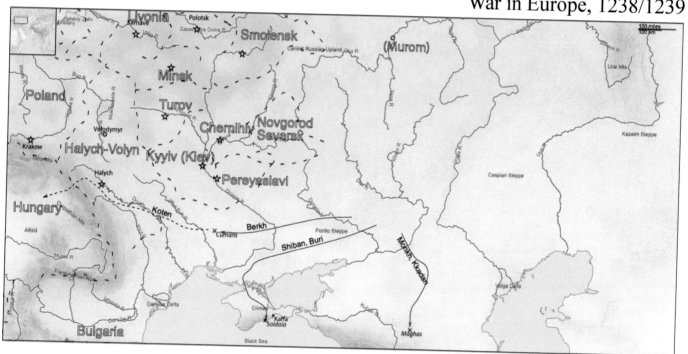

Later in 1238 and early 1239, the Mongols sent out armies against the lesser enemies that still remained on the steppe. Monkh and Khadan were dispatched against the Alans and took their stronghold Maghas. Shiban and Buri went into Crimea and took the Genoese outpost of Soldaia again. Berkh moved west against the Cumans. One of their leaders, Koten, fled with his people and sought refuge in Hungary. [32]

War with Song China, 1239

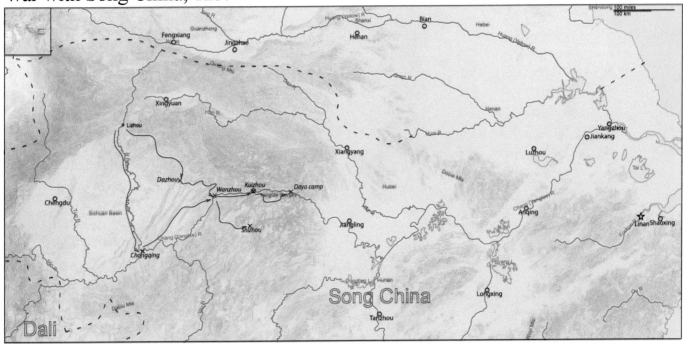

The Mongols moved south again from Lizhou and attacked Chongqing. Another column moved against Wanzhou and both combined to attack towards Kuizhou. The Mongols pressed on further east from Kuizhou but were turned back at Daya Camp. [33]

War in the Middle East, 1239

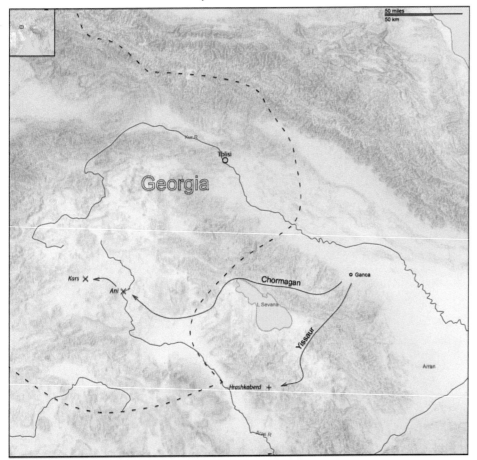

Chormagan advanced further west, taking Ani and Kars. Yissaur moved south to invest Hrashkaberd which surrendered. [34]

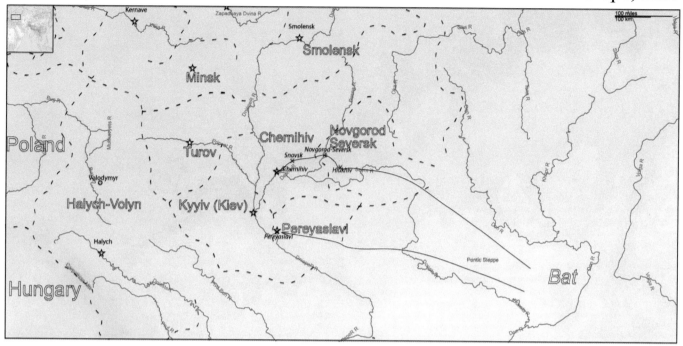

There were two separate advances against the southern Rus in 1239. One attacked Perieslavl which was taken on March 3. Six months later the Mongols moved against Chernihiv along the Seim and Desna Rivers. Chernihiv was taken on October 18. Following both moves the Mongols returned to the Pontic Steppe. [35]

Expedition to Tibet, 1240

From his camp near Lake Qinghai, Godan sent Doorda Darkhan on an expedition into Tibet. This was a reconnaissance mission more than anything since Tibet was unknown territory to the Mongols. There was minimal conflict, but two monasteries were burned. [36]

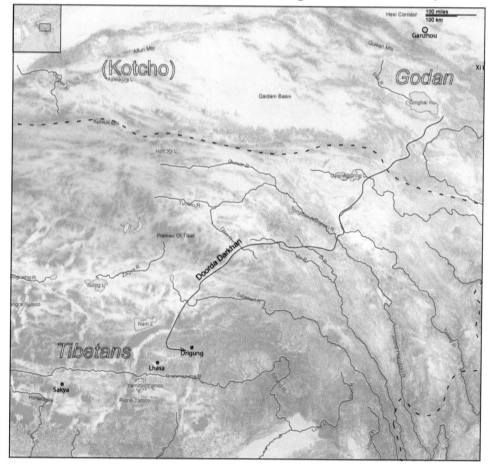

War in Europe, Winter 1240/1241

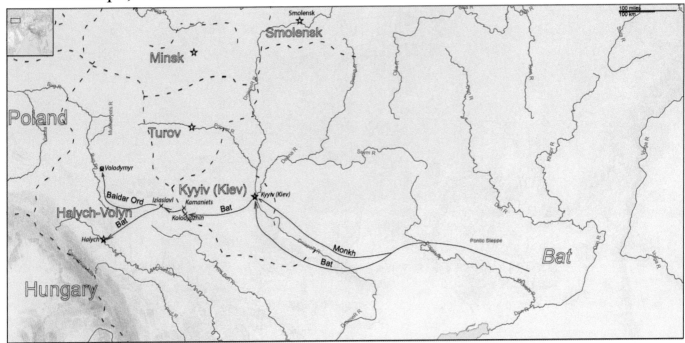

After resting his forces for an entire year, Bat advanced on Kyyiv (Kiev) in November. The advance force under Monkh arrived to demand the surrender, but the Mongol envoys were killed. Bat arrived later and the city was taken on December 6 after a nine day siege. Bat then advanced against Halych-Volyn in January. Prince Danylo had fled as the Mongols approached. By February, Bat had reached Halych and a force under Baidar had reached Volodymyr. Both cities were quickly taken. [37]

War in Europe, Winter/Spring 1241

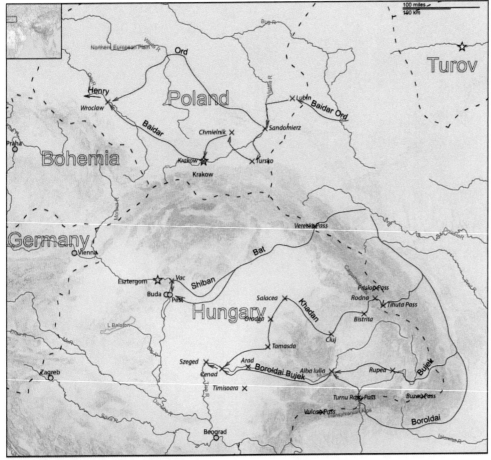

Wasting no time, Bat moved against Hungary and Poland. He divided his main force to invade Hungary. Bat himself and Subeedei pushed through the Verecke Pass and on to Pest. Shiban, leading the advance force, took Vac and reunited with Bat at Pest on March 17. Khadan, Bujek, and Boroldai went south. They also pushed through the mountains and took many towns before meeting up at Cenad. The northern force moving into Poland also split up. Baidar went southwest while Ord went northwest. Baidar defeated Polish armies at Tursko and Chmielnik and took the capital, Krakow, on March 24. He reunited with Ord at Wroclaw. Henry of Silesia had left Wroclaw to assemble an army just to the west. [38]

In Poland, Baidar and Ord decisively defeated Henry of Silesia at Legnica on April 9. Wenceslaw of Bohemia had begun moving to join Henry but was too late. After Legnica, Baidar and Ord turned south to join Bat in Hungary. King Bela of Hungary had assembled his army at Buda. Bat retreated east, tempting Bela to follow. When Bela did so, Bat turned and decisively defeated him at Mohi on April 11. Bela fled first to Vienna and then fled south, Bat moved back to Pest. [39]

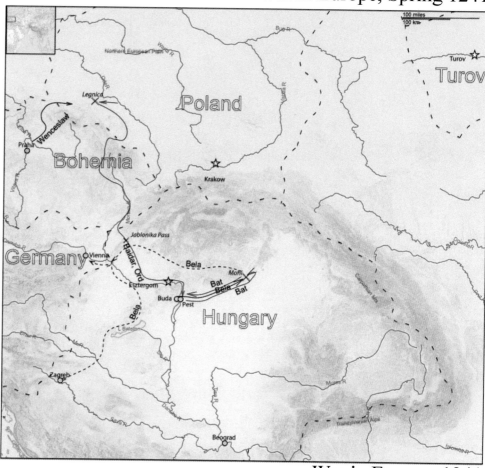

During the summer the Mongols sent raiding and reconnaissance parties out in all directions, but the army did not cross the Danube River until December when it froze over. Khadan was sent with an augmented force to pursue Bela, then at Zagreb. Bela fled further south as the Mongols approached and Khadan followed. Bat also crossed and attacked the Hungarian capital, Esztergom, taking it on December 25. Around this time, the news reached Bat that Ogedei had died on December 11. [40]

War with Song China, 1241

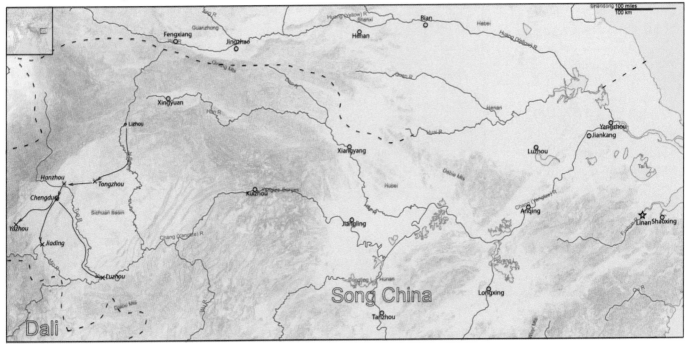

Another Mongol effort was made in the Sichuan region in late 1241. Hanzhou and Chengdu were captured but other raids sent out from there were unsuccessful. [41]

Invasion of India, 1241

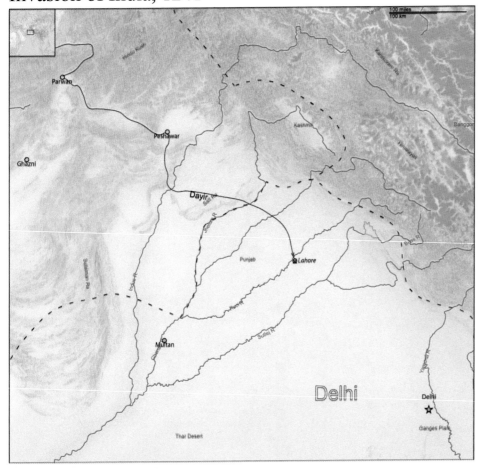

Dayir was ordered into India in late 1241. He besieged the city of Lahore but was killed in the assault in December. Munggetu sacked the city and returned with the army to Persia. [42]

Guyug, 1242-1248

Countries & Peoples – 1/1/1242

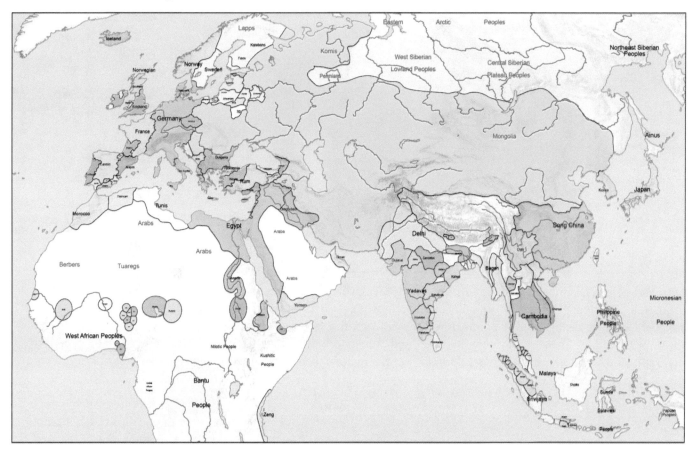

Some principal events between 1228 and 1242.

Africa. New: Mali c1240, Tlemcen and Tunis from Morocco 1236

Western Europe. New: Grenada, Jaen, Murcia, Seville, and Valencia from Morocco 1233. Holy Roman Empire-Papacy war 1228-1241. Mongolia conquered Hungary and Poland 1241-1242.

Eastern Europe. Bulgaria-Epirus war 1230. Mongolia conquered most Rus principalities 1236-1241. Novgorod submitted to Mongolia 1238.

Middle East. Mongolia conquered Persia 1230-1239.

Central Asia. Ogedei installed as Great Khan 1229.

Eastern Asia. Mongolia-Jin China war 1228-1234. Mongolia-Korea war 1231-1238. Mongolia-Song China war 1236-1241.

Southern Asia. New: Bengal from Delhi 1241. Yadavas took Kadamba 1238. Assam replaced Kamarupa 1229.

South-Eastern Asia. New: Sukhothai from Haripunjaya 1238.

Regency of Turkhan, 1242 to 1246

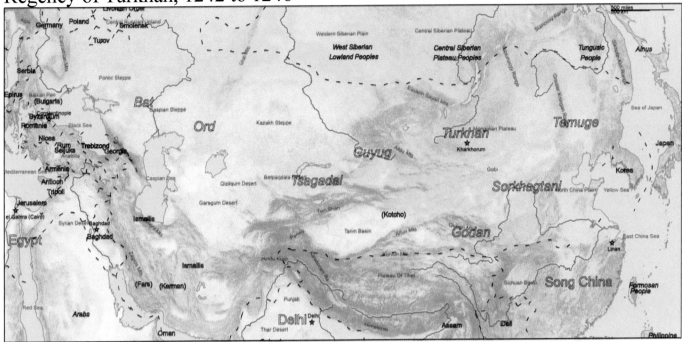

Ogedei died on December 11, 1241 at Kharkhorum. His favorite son, Khuchu, had died in 1236. Khuchu's son, Shiremun, was still young. Ogedei's widow, Turkhan, became regent with the support of Tsagadai, and would lobby for her son, Guyug, to be the next Great Khan. However due to conflict between Guyug and Bat, there was no consensus in the imperial family. The sons of Zuchi, Bat, Ord, and Shiban, opposed Guyug. Tului's widow, Sorkhagtani, professed neutrality and bided her time. Her son, Monkh, was Bat's friend. Temujin's brother, Temuge, had plans of his own. [1]

War in Europe, 1242

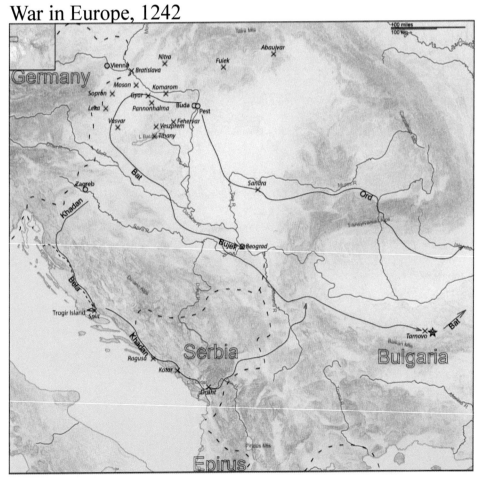

News of Ogedei's death did not put a stop to operations in the west. The Mongols raided all over western Hungary, but many fortified places held out. Not wanting to commit to lengthy sieges, Bat began to move back east. Bujek took Belgrade as the Mongols passed by. Ord collected the forces in eastern Hungary and also moved east. Bela of Hungary had fled from Zagreb when Khadan approached. He continued moving from place to place along the Adriatic Sea. Khadan almost caught him at Split but Bela escaped to the island of Trogir. Just as in Korea, the Mongols could not cross the deep water. Khadan then turned east and met up with Bat in Bulgaria in the spring. The Bulgarians inflicted a minor defeat on the advance force, but the main force came up and took Tarnovo. Bulgaria agreed to submit. Bat then led his army back to the steppes. [2]

The war with Song China also continued after Ogedei's death, although it was not pursued with the same energy. Several raids were made in the Sichuan region. Another thrust was made to Tungzhou in the east, near the mouth of the Chang (Yangtze) River. In 1243, Yu Jie was appointed Song commissioner in Sichuan based at Chongqing. He began to construct a network of fortifications. [3]

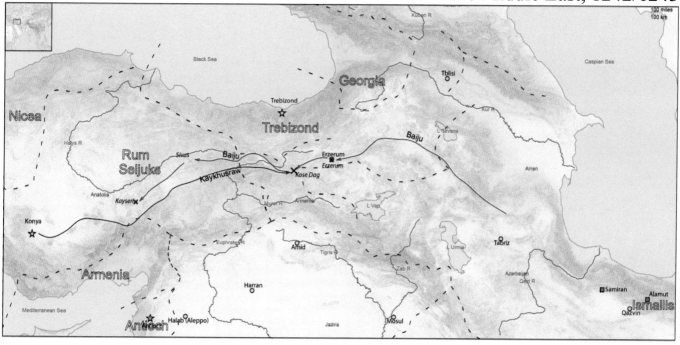

After Ogedei's death, Baiju began to pressure Kaykhusraw II, the Seljuk Sultan of Rum, to go to Mongolia to make his submission. When the Sultan resisted, Baiju invaded, taking Erzerum in the winter. Kaykhusraw marched against the Mongols but was soundly defeated at Kose Dag on June 26, 1243. Baiju continued on to Sivas and Kayseri and Kaykhusraw was forced to submit. Trebizond and Armenia, which had supported Kaykhusraw, also submitted. Queen Rusudan of Georgia also accepted the inevitable and submitted. [4]

Consolidation in the West, 1242/1243

While Subeedei, many of the princes, and parts of the army returned to Mongolia, Bat and his brothers remained in the west to consolidate their power. Bat established his camp at Sarai and began to build a city. Without the support of a unified empire, no further campaigns in Europe could be considered. Bat summoned the surviving Rus princes to Sarai to formally submit and be invested as subject rulers. [5]

War with Song China, 1244/1245

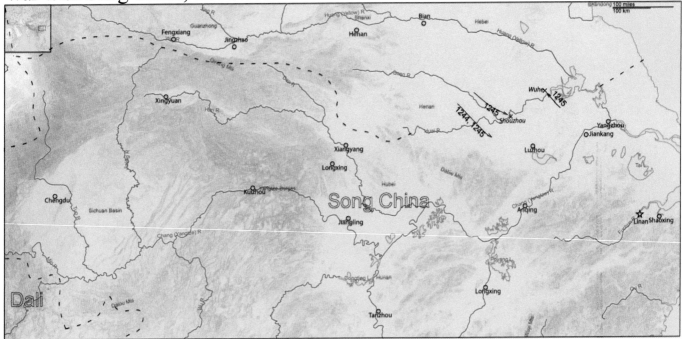

The Mongols continued to raid south of the Huai River. Song forces counterattacked at Wuhe in 1244. The Mongols occupied Shouzhou in 1245. [6]

In 1244, Khadan summoned the Lama Pandita from the Sakya monastery to his camp as a prelude to extending Mongol control over Tibet. Pandita arrived in 1246 along with his nephews, Phagpa and Chakna Dorje. [7]

Relations with Tibet, 1244/1246

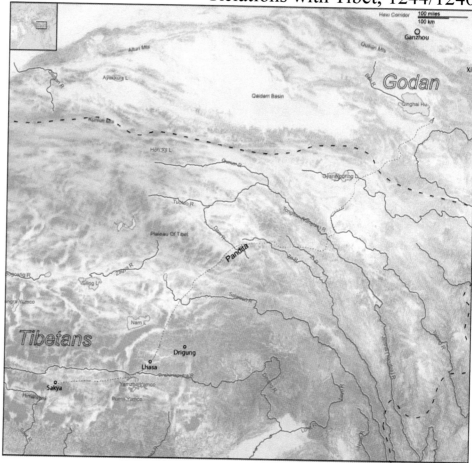

The Mongols invaded India once again in the winter, this time led by Munggetu. He captured Multan and besieged Uch but withdrew as a Delhi army approached. [8]

Invasion of India, 1245/1246

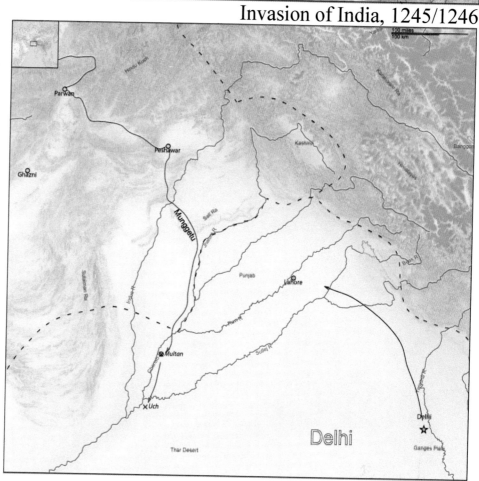

War with Song China, 1246/1247

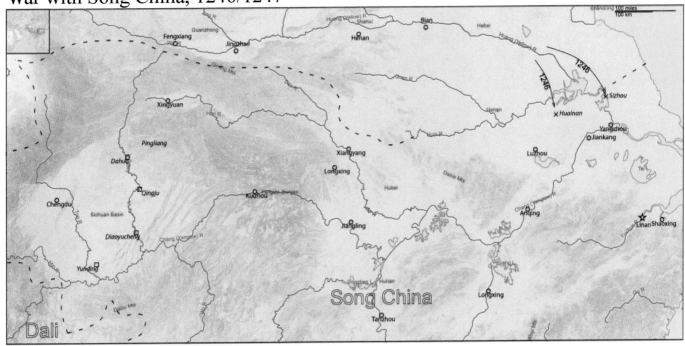

Guyug was formally installed as Great Khan on August 24, 1246 at Kharkhorum. Subjects and ambassadors from all over the world were in attendance. Bat would not go himself, but he did send his brothers. The Mongols continued to concentrate on the Huai River region. As they did so, Yu Jie was restoring Song positions and building fortifications in Sichuan.[9]

War with Korea, 1247/1248

Seeing that the Koreans had still not removed their court from Ganghwa Island, Guyug sent Amugan with a force to once again try to enforce the terms of Korea's surrender. Amugan arrived at Yomju in the fall of 1247 and sent out raiding parties from there. As before, the Mongols could move unopposed anywhere in the country but could not reach Ganghwa. Amugan would return to Mongolia after Guyug's death.[10]

Guyug had repeatedly summoned Bat to Kharkhorum to make his submission, but Bat ignored the summons. Finally, Guyug decided to force the issue and marched from Kharkhorum with an army in the fall of 1247. Bat also moved to meet him with an army. Open war was only averted when Guyug died on April 20, 1248 at Khum Sengir. Bat had reached Ala Khamag by that time. [11]

Monkh 1248 to 1259

Countries & Peoples – 1/1/1249

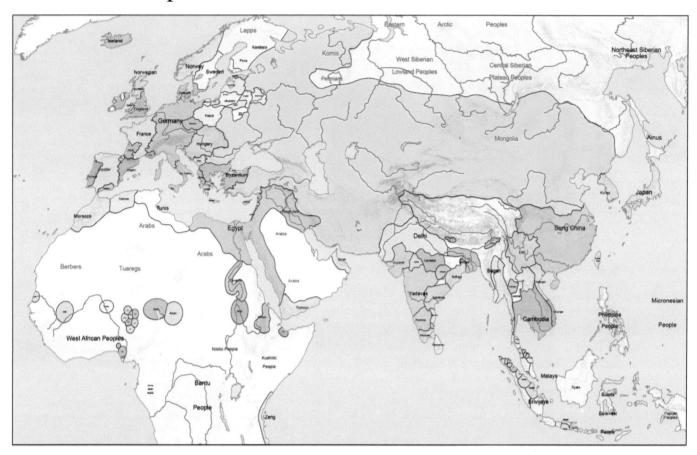

Some principal events between 1242 and 1249.

Africa. No significant events.

Western Europe. New: Provence from Germany 1246. Mongolia withdrew from Hungary and Poland 1242. England-France war 1242-1243. Holy Roman Empire-Papacy war 1243-1250. Castile took Murcia 1243, Jaen 1246, Seville 1248. Aragon took Valencia 1246.

Eastern Europe. Bat consolidated Mongol rule 1242-1243. Byzantium reestablished 1246.

Middle East. Mongolia-Rum war 1242-1243, Rum, Armenia, Trebizond, and Georgia submitted to Mongolia 1242-1243.

Central Asia. Guyug installed as Great Khan 1246.

Eastern Asia. Mongolia-Song China war 1242-1247. Mongolia-Korea war 1247-1248.

Southern Asia. Bengal took Senas 1245

South-Eastern Asia. No significant events.

Regency of Ogul Khaimish, 1248 to 1251

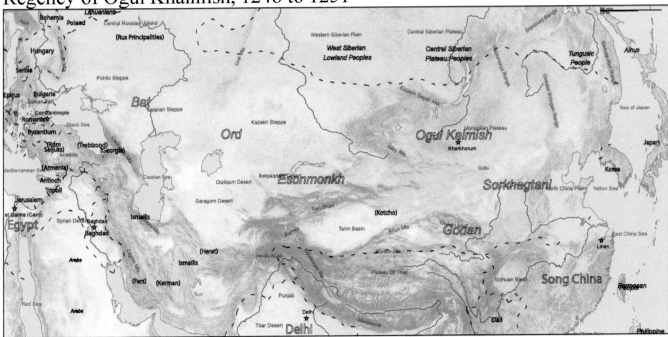

Guyug's widow, Ogul Khaimish, was named regent. However Bat, in his camp at Ala Khamag, called an assembly which proclaimed Monkh as the new Great Khan. This was not held in the Mongol homeland and was boycotted by most of the princes in Ogedei's and Tsagadai's line. Ogedei's family could not agree between one of Guyug's two sons or their cousin Shiremun. In 1251, Bat called for another assembly at Kharkhorum and sent Berkh along with an army to enforce his choice. Monkh was proclaimed again and subsequently purged all those who had not supported him. [1]

War in Europe, 1252

Guyug had appointed Andrey Vladimirevich as prince of Vladimir. When Andrey tried to assert his independence, Bat's son, Sartag, led a punitive expedition against Vladimir. Andrey was defeated at Perieslav-Zalesky and fled to Sweden. Bat appointed Andrey's brother, Alexander Vladimirevich, in his place. [2]

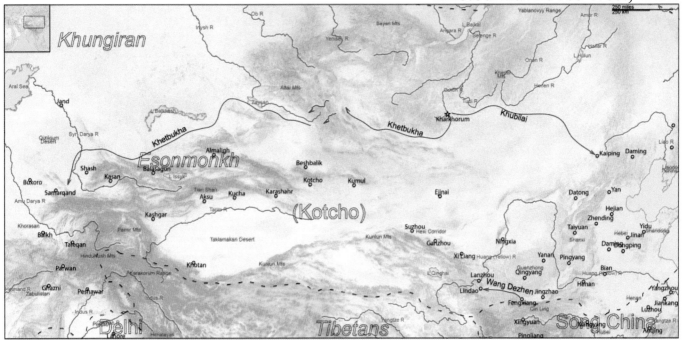

Once the purges were over, Monkh resolved to resume Mongol expansion. Two areas were designated as prime objectives. The first was Song China where Monkh put his brother, Khubilai, in charge. Khubilai established his headquarters at Kaiping and sent Wang Dezhen to make a base of operations at Lindao. The second was the Middle East where the Ismailis and the Caliph at Baghdad were still independent. Monkh's brother, Khulegu, was placed in command and forces were gathered. Khetbukha moved west with Khulegu's advance force in the summer. Monkh also appointed Tsagadai's grandson, Khara Khulegu, to replace Guyug's appointee, Esonmonkh, as head of Tsagadai's Domain. [3]

Expedition to Tibet, 1252/1253

One of the few princes in Ogedei's line to survive the purges was Khadan, who had supported Monkh. From his camp near Lake Qinghai, Khadan sent another expedition to Tibet under Khoridai. [4]

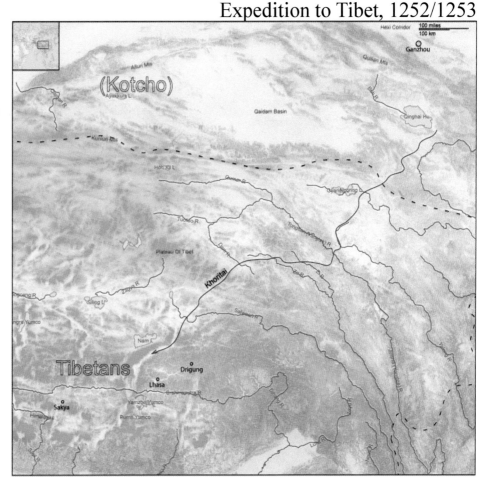

War with the Ismailis, 1253

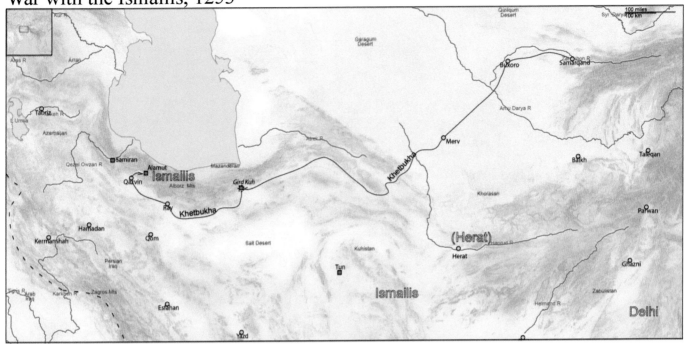

Khetbukha crossed the Amu Darya River in March and proceeded to invest the Ismaili fortress of Gird Kuh in May. Leaving a force there to blockade, he moved on in August to raid Alamut. Returning to Gird Kuh, he settled in for a siege. [5]

War with Dali, 1253

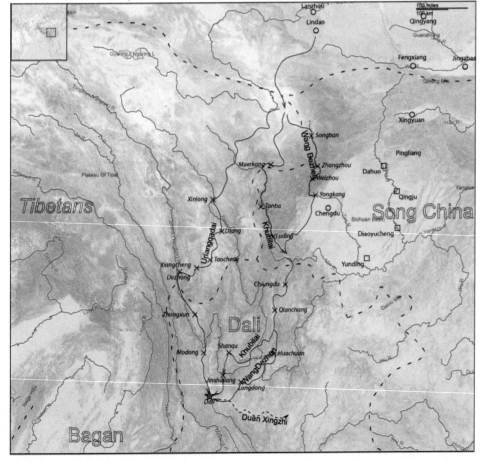

Khubilai's force moved south from Lindao in September 1253 and split up after the first month. Khubilai commanded the center himself, Uriangkhadai led the right wing, and Wang Dezhen the left. There was little resistance except from the difficult mountain terrain. A Dali army formed up on the south bank of the Jinsha (Yangtze) River but was defeated. Khubilai advanced on the Dali capital in December and was joined there by Uriangkhadai and Wang Dezhen. The ruler of Dali, Duan Xingzhi, fled and the city surrendered. [6]

Monkh discovered that the prince the Koreans had sent as a hostage in 1238 was not the crown prince but only a distant relative. That and the continued Korean refusal to leave Ganghwa Island led to yet another Mongol invasion. After sending several envoys, Yeku crossed the Yalu River in August and moved south. The mountain fortress of Chongju was able to withstand a siege but elsewhere the Mongols rode freely. In the spring of 1254, Yeku was recalled and the Mongols withdrew once again. [7]

Khulegu Moves West, 1253/1255

Khulegu began moving with his main force in May 1253. Monkh gave him a huge send-off. He celebrated more at his own camp in September. Reaching Almaligh in 1254, he was further feasted by Urgana, regent for her son Mubarak Shah. He camped nearby in the mountains for the summer. Khulegu did not reach Samarqand until September 1255. [8]

War with Dali, 1254 to 1256

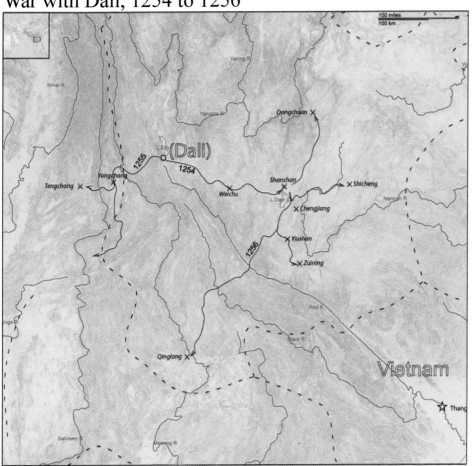

Khubilai returned to Kaiping early in 1254, leaving Uriangkhadai in command, but the war was not over. Duan Xingzhi had fled to Shanchan and many of the subordinate tribes were not ready to submit either. Uriangkhadai's first task was to capture Duan Xingzhi. Uriangkhadai advanced on Shanchan in 1254, but Duàn Xingzhi fled again. He was tracked down and captured shortly however. Following that, Uriangkhadai fanned out subduing local tribes. In 1255 he campaigned in the west and in 1256 he turned south. Duan Xingzhi was sent to Monkh in 1255. There he became reconciled with the Mongols and returned as their subject ruler. [9]

War with Korea, 1254 to 1259

In 1254, Monkh appointed Jalairtai to deal with the Koreans. Jalairtai began a relentless series of invasions which reached all parts of the peninsula. By 1258, Korea was in ruins. However, it was a coup on Ganghwa Island that finally resolved the situation. Throughout the conflict with Korea, the Choe family, with their private army, had been the main obstacle to peace. In 1258, one of the Choe retainers assassinated Choe Ui, the new head of the family, and restored the king to power. The Koreans sued for peace and this time the offer was genuine. Peace was concluded in April 1259 and the real crown prince set out for Mongolia. Work began dismantling the fortifications on Ganghwa and restoring the old capital for use. [10]

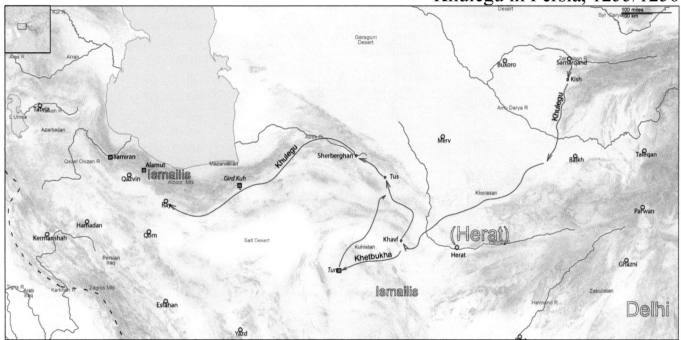

Khulegu reached Samarqand in the fall of 1255. In November, he was at Kish where he summoned subject rulers from all over Persia to renew their submission. Crossing the Amu Darya River at the end of the year he stopped to hunt. Khulegu next moved toward the Ismailis. He stopped at Khavf where Khetbukha was detached to take the Ismaili fortress of Tun. Khetbukha rejoined Khulegu at Tus where another month was spent celebrating. Spending the summer in the mountains near Sherbergan, Khulegu began negotiating a surrender with Kurshah, the new Grand Master of the Ismailis. As negotiations dragged on, Khulegu moved to Ray in September and began to prepare an assault. [11]

War with the Ismailis, 1256

Kurshah's resolve had already been weakened by Khulegu's diplomacy. Khulegu next showed overwhelming force as his army converged from three directions on Maimun Diz, the current Ismaili headquarters. Bokhtomor and Koke Ilge led the right column, Balaghai and Tutar commanded the left, Khulegu himself led the center and Khetbukha brought up the rear. Khulegu marched directly over the mountains and almost captured the fortress by surprise on November 8. Negotiations continued and Kurshah was promised amnesty for all if he would surrender himself and all the other fortresses. After a brief bombardment, Kurshah surrendered on November 19, and all the nearby fortresses, except Lammasar, followed suit. [12]

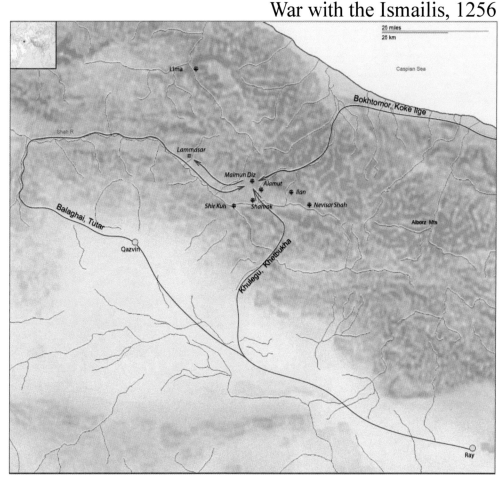

War with Baghdad, 1257

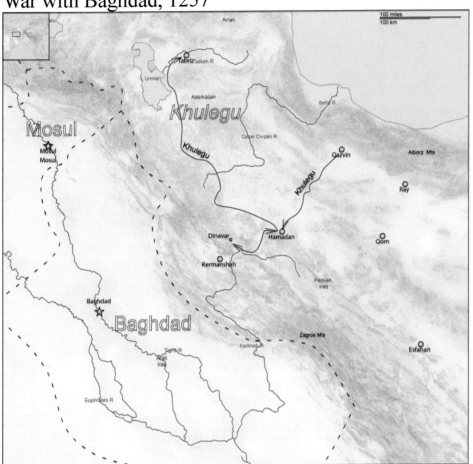

After the surrender of the Ismailis, Khulegu moved on to Hamadan which he reached by April. From there he began negotiations with Mustasim, the Caliph at Baghdad. Mustasim was willing to pay tribute but not offer unconditional submission. Khulegu advanced as far as Dinavar but returned to Hamadan when it became clear Mustasim would not submit. By July, Khulegu had moved to Tabriz to organize his forces for an invasion. [13]

War with Song China, 1257

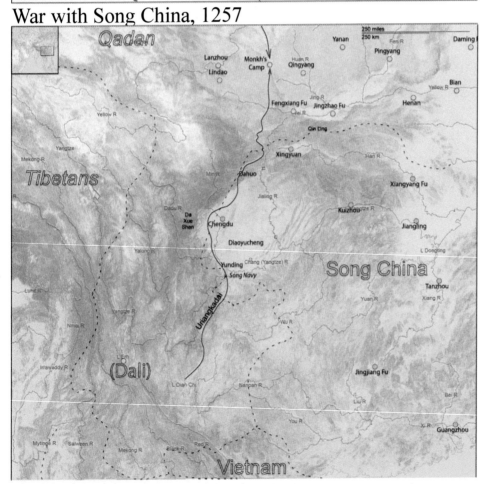

In May 1257, Monkh began assembling an army to prepare for war with Song China. Uriangkhadai was recalled from Dali. On the way north, he encountered a Song force that included 200 ships on the upper Chang (Yangtze) River. He defeated it and captured or destroyed the ships. In the fall of 1257, Uriangkhadai returned to Dali with orders to subdue Vietnam. [14]

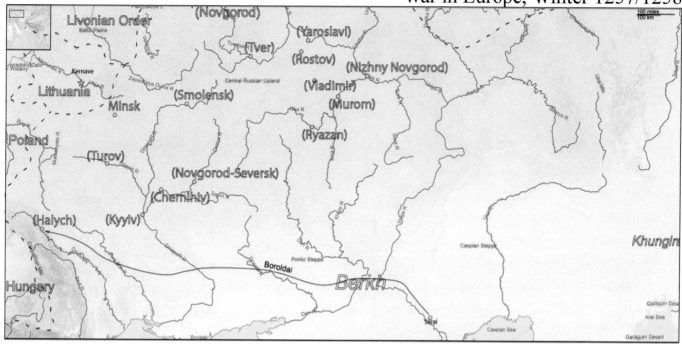

Despite his initial submission to the Mongols, Prince Danylo of Halych had resumed relations with Poland and Hungary and began to resist Mongol tax collectors and governors. In 1254, he had attempted to seize Kyyiv (Kiev) for himself. In 1257, Berkh sent Boroldai to bring Danylo back into line. When Boroldai arrived and ordered him to dismantle all his fortifications or face destruction, Danylo complied. [15]

War with Vietnam, Winter 1257/1258

Late in 1257, Uriangkhadai began moving down the Red River Valley. Vietnam assembled an army which included elephants, but the Mongols defeated it and took the capital, Thang Long. The Vietnamese emperor fled to an offshore island. However, in January he returned and counterattacked. Uriangkhadai retreated back to Dali. [16]

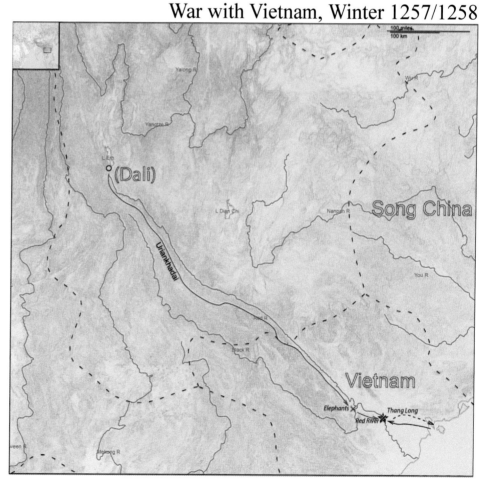

War with Baghdad, Fall/Winter 1257/1258

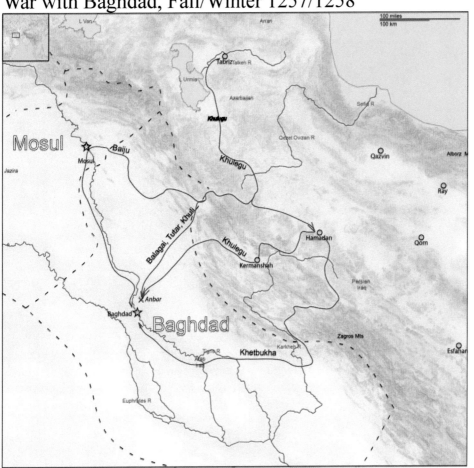

By the fall of 1257, Khulegu was ready. He divided his force into four columns and they set out, timed to converge on Baghdad at the end of the year. Khetbukha led the left wing, moving south through the Zagros Mountains and then turning west to attack from the southeast. Baiju turned west and crossed the Tigris River at Mosul. The local ruler submitted and Baiju continued south to attack Baghdad from the northwest. Khulegu moved in the center with a right wing commanded by Balagai, Tutar, and Khuli on a parallel course. Early in January, they were confronted by the Baghdad army at Anbar and defeated it. The columns then converged on the city of Baghdad. [17]

Siege of Baghdad, Winter 1258

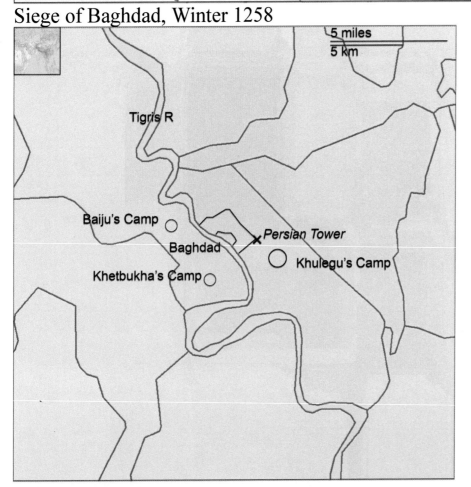

The siege of Baghdad began on January 29. The Mongols surrounded the city with siege works and brought up machines. On February 4, they breached the walls at the Persian Tower. Mustasim attempted one last negotiation but was ignored. He surrendered on February 10 and the Mongols entered the city four days later. Mustasim was executed later in February and a Mongol governor was installed. Khulegu and most of the army returned to Azerbaijan in late spring. [18]

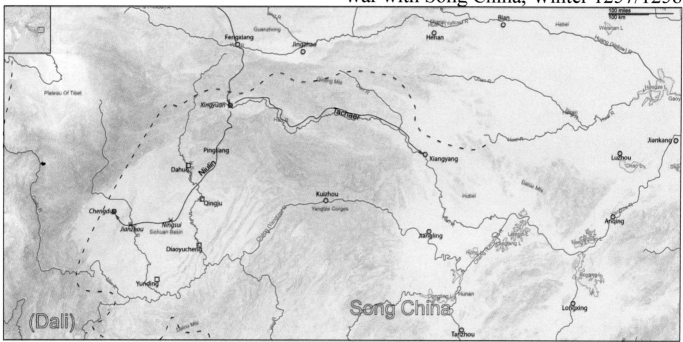

Monkh's invasion of Song China began with the advance force moving south to Xingyang. From there, one group went west, bypassing the major fortresses, to Chengdu. Chengdu fell to the Mongols in February. The other group turned east and moved down the Han River Valley. Their objective was Fancheng, the twin city of Xiangyang. [19]

In December 1257, Khulegu sent Sali to invade India. He defeated the ruler of Multan and dismantled the defenses. Khulegu had ordered him not to infringe on Delhi's territory, however, and he withdrew. [20]

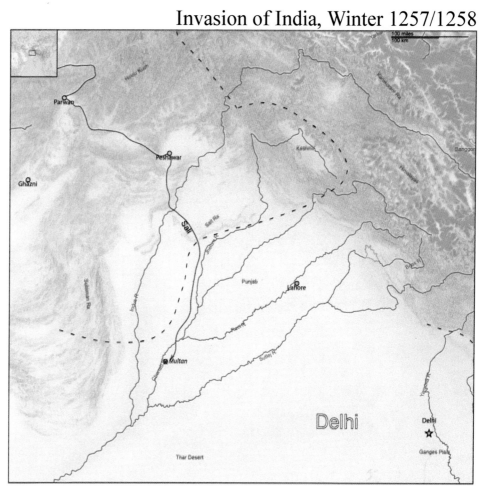

War with Song China, 1258

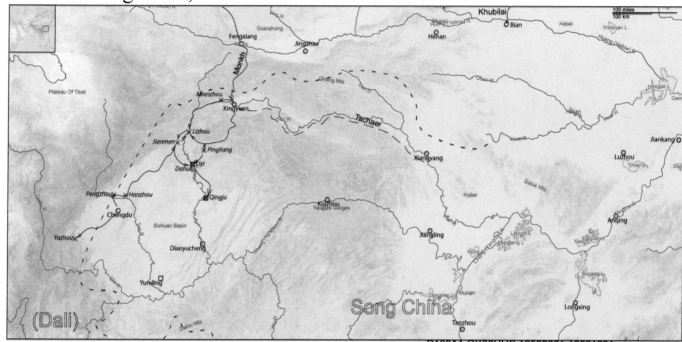

P100A1 GK08HUS 12580601-12581231.png

Monkh moved south with his main force in June. His first objective was Lizhou. The column from Chengdu also advanced moving north. The Mongols won a victory at Jianmen and encircled Lizhou, which fell in October. Monkh advanced further south to the Dahuo and Qingju fortresses and they fell as well. Other parts of the plan were also set in motion. Khubilai advanced south from Kaiping and Uriangkhadai began to move east from Dali. The column that had advanced to Fancheng, however, turned back because of bad weather. [21]

War in Europe, Winter 1258/1259

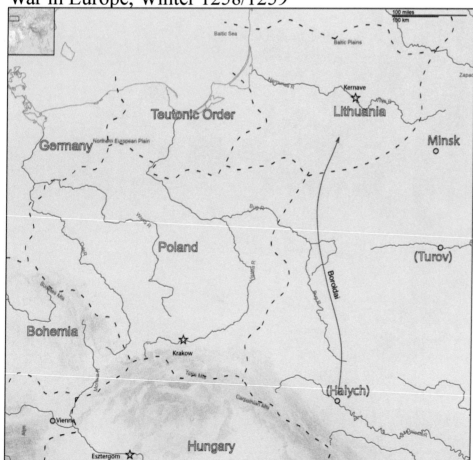

From Halych, Boroldai marched north to attack Lithuania, which had been raiding Mongol territory. Minsk had also turned to Lithuania for help against the Mongols. The Lithuanian army did not offer resistance. After raiding some towns and villages, Boroldai returned to Halych. [22]

After spending some time in the north, Monkh returned to the front and led his army to Diaoyucheng, a major fortress opposite the city of Hezhou. He arrived there in February. The Song defender, Wang Jian, was determined to resist and a siege began. A Song relief force came up the Chang (Yangtze) River but was turned back. During the siege, the force from Chengdu moved south to Luzhou and then on towards Chongqing. It was stopped at Fuzhou. Khubilai's column was also on the move. He crossed the Huai River in August. Uriangkhadai approached from the south following the Xiang River, and approached Tanzhou. [3]

Siege of Diaoyucheng, 1259

Diaoyucheng was mostly surrounded by the Jialing, Qu, and Fu Rivers, with walls extending from the fortress to the riverbanks. The defenders were well supplied and determined. While direct assaults failed, the Mongols were able to break through the northern extension and surround the fortress on all sides. However, they could not achieve a further breakthrough. As the siege dragged on into the summer, disease spread in the Mongol camp. Among the victims was Monkh himself. He died on August 11. [24]

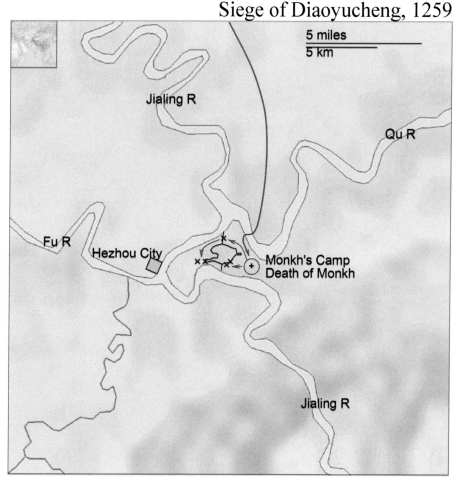

Khubilai, 1259 to 1279

Countries & Peoples – 1/1/1260

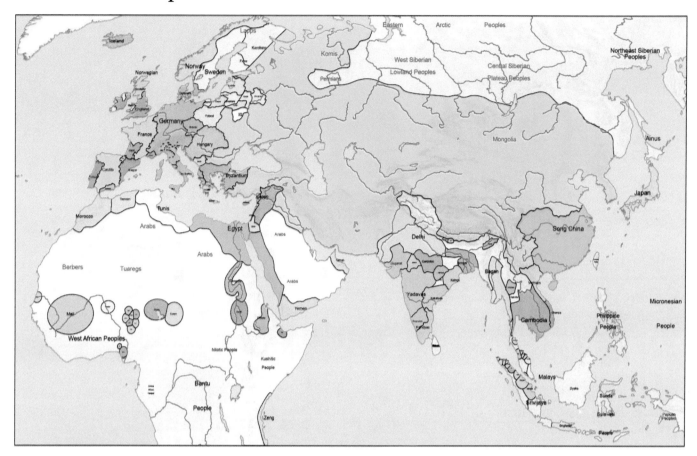

Some principal events between 1249 and 1260.

Africa. Mali expanded c 1255.

Western Europe. Italian cities established independence after 1250. Sweden and Norway expanded northwards c1250.

Eastern Europe. No significant events.

Middle East. New: Halab (Aleppo), Kerak, and Mosul from Egypt after Mamluk soldiers deposed the Ayyubid dynasty 1250. Mongolia-Ismaili war 1253-1256. Mongolia-Baghdad war 1257-1258, Mosul submitted 1257, Baghdad conquered 1258.

Central Asia. Monkh installed as Great Khan 1251.

Eastern Asia. Mongolia-Dali war 1253-1256. Mongolia-Korea war 1253-1259. Mongolia-Song China war 1257-1260, Mongolia-Vietnam war 1257-1258.

Southern Asia. No significant events.

South-Eastern Asia. Singhasari took Janggala and Panjalu 1254.

War with Song China, Fall/Winter 1259/1260

Monkh's son, Asutai, escorted his father's body back to Mongolia. Khubilai reached the Chang (Yangtze) River in September and crossed in October to meet up with Uriangkhadai, who had moved north after taking Tanzhou. They began to besiege Ezhou. Song China sent envoys to Khubilai offering a truce, but he rejected the offer. [1]

War in Europe, Winter 1259/1260

Boroldai continued his punishment of Danylo of Halych by invading Poland. Danylo had relied on Poland for support of his independence efforts. Now he was forced to participate against Poland. Boroldai advanced in December and laid siege to Sandomierz. While the siege was underway, columns were sent out to raid the countryside. Sandomierz fell on February 2 and Boroldai advanced on Krakow. The Mongols quickly captured the city, but the citadel held out and the Mongols withdrew. [2]

War in the Middle East, Fall/Winter 1259

After resting for the summer, Khulegu resumed his push west. Khetbukha led the advance force, Shikhtur and Baiju the right wing, and Sunchakh the left wing. Khulegu himself led the center and departed from Tabriz on September 12. Mayyafariqin resisted for some time and Khulegu left his son, Eshmed, to finish the job, as the main army moved on. The columns converged on Halab (Aleppo) by the end of the year. Khulegu did not make any move to return to Mongolia after receiving the news of Monkh's death. [3]

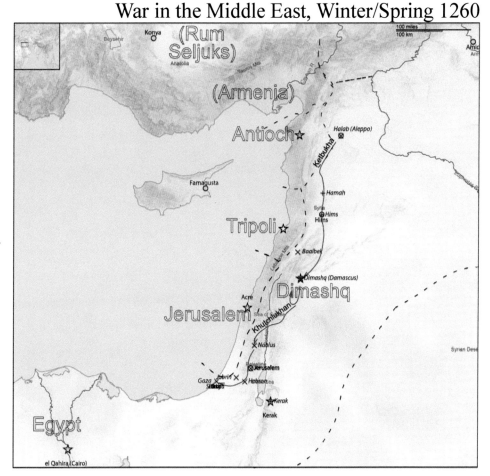

War in the Middle East, Winter/Spring 1260

Halab (Aleppo) fell on January 24, although the citadel held out until February 25. Khulegu sent Khetbukha south to Hama, Hims, and Dimashq (Damascus), each of which surrendered without opposition (Dimashq on March 1). Khetbukha continued south but had to turn back, when rebels seized the citadel at Dimashq. They held out there until April 28. When Khetbukha turned back, he left Kushlukhan to continue south. Kushlukhan defeated a read guard at Nablus then his force spread out. raiding as far as Kerak, which submitted, and Gaza. Baidar remained at Gaza. In the meantime, with summer approaching, Khulegu moved back to Azerbaijan with most of his army, just as he had done after the fall of Baghdad. He passed north of Lake Van in June. [4]

Arigbokh and Khubilai, Spring 1260

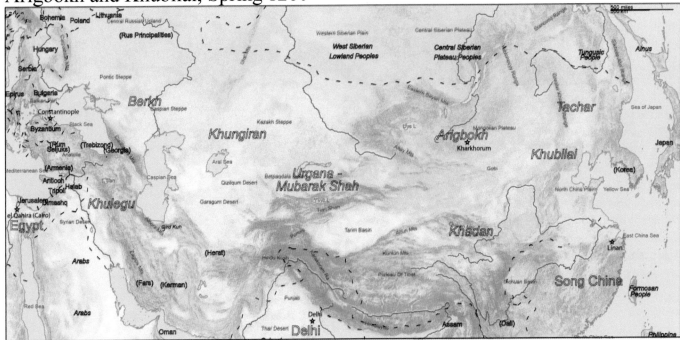

When Monkh died there was no strong regent, like Turkhan, to take control, nor was there a kingmaker, like Bat, who could enforce his choice. Monkh also left two brothers who would not yield to the other. None of the regional princes made any move to return to Mongolia. Arigbokh and Khubilai began to gather supporters and maneuver for position. In January, Khubilai abandoned the siege of Ezhou and returned to his base at Kaiping. He was proclaimed Great Khan by his supporters there in May. Arigbokh, at Kharkhorum, was proclaimed Great Khan in June. Only their close supporters attended either assembly. [5]

War in the Middle East, Fall/Winter 1260

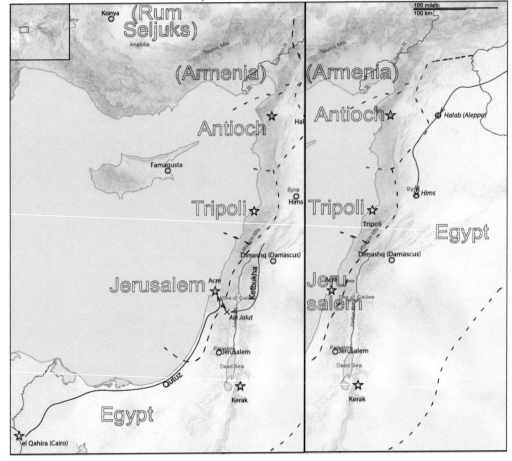

Qutuz, Sultan of Egypt since November 1259, decided to take advantage of Khulegu's absence to confront Khetbukha in Syria. He left El Qahira (Cairo) in July, 1260. Baidar withdrew from Gaza as Qutuz approached. Qutuz continued to advance, pausing at Acre. Khetbukha moved south from Baalbek and crossed the Jordan River. The two armies met at Ain Jalut on September 3. The Mongols were defeated and Khetbukha was killed. The cities of Syria reverted to Egyptian control and Qutuz returned to Egypt. In November, Khulegu sent a small force under Ilge to recover the lost territory. Ilge retook Halab (Aleppo) but was defeated by local forces at Hims on December 10. [6]

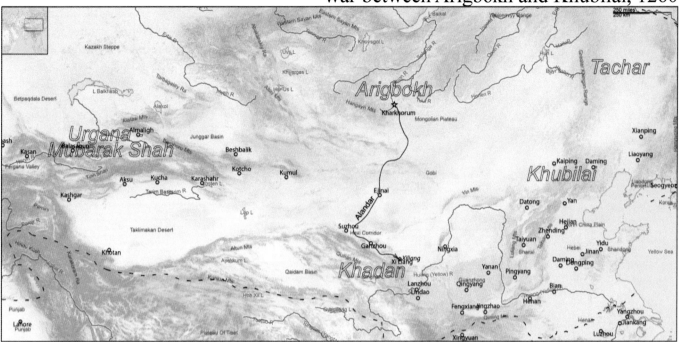

As the year progressed, the major princes chose sides. Most of Monkh's family, the court at Kharkhorum, Berkh and Khungiran supported Arigbokh. Khulegu, Khadan, and Tachar supported Khubilai. Urgana, in the Tsagadai territories, tried to remain neutral so both Arigbokh and Khubilai appointed rival princes to take over her territory. Arigbokh sent Alandar to take over the Hexi corridor. Khubilai sent Lian Xixian to Jingzhao to secure Guanzhong and gain the support of Monkh's army, still in the field. Khadan defeated Alandar at Xiliang and Lian Xixian was successful in his mission. Both were handsomely rewarded by Khubilai. [7]

War between Arigbokh and Khubilai, 1261

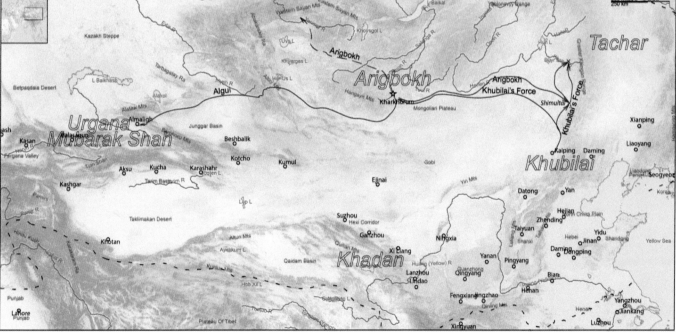

Arigbokh's appointee, Algui, was able to depose Urgana and take over the Tsagadai territories. Khubilai's appointee for that task, Abishka, was captured by Arigbokh and later executed. In November, the armies of Arigbokh and Khubilai clashed in eastern Mongolia near the Khingan Mountains. Arigbokh was defeated at Shimultai in the first battle. Even though a second battle was indecisive, Arigbokh withdrew to the Upper Yenisey Valley and Khubilai's forces advanced to occupy Kharkhorum. [8]

Rebellion in the Middle East, 1261/1262

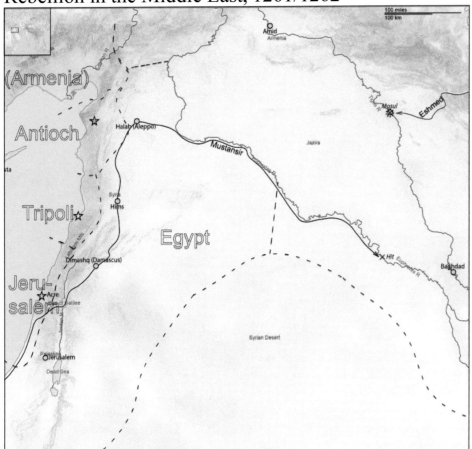

The ruler of Mosul who had submitted in 1257, died in 1261, and his son rebelled against the Mongols. Khulegu sent his son, Eshmed, to deal with this. Egypt tried to support the rebellion and recover Baghdad in the process. Mustansir led an army through Syria and down the Euphrates River, only to be defeated at Hit by local Mongol forces. Mosul held out under siege for over a year before it fell. [9]

War with Song China, 1261 to 1264

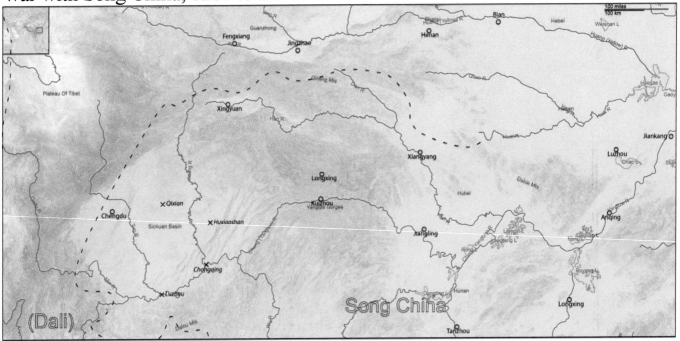

The Mongols were still in control of large parts of Sichuan. Song forces attacked Luzhou in June 1261. In 1262, they captured it and also retook Qixian. In 1263, there was an indecisive battle at Chongqing, and in 1264, another one at Huxiaoshan. [10]

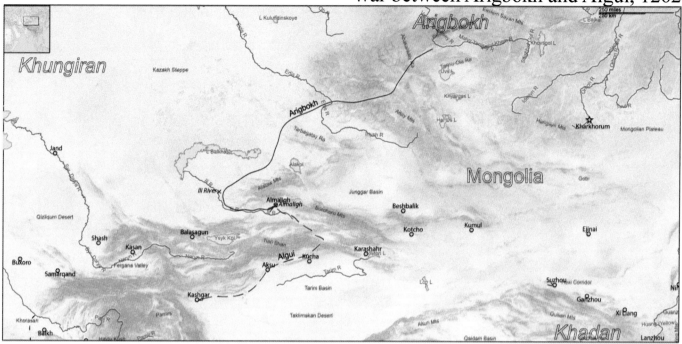

In 1262, Algui broke with his patron, Arigbokh, and war followed. Arigbokh's advance force lost a battle along the Ili River but the main army succeeded in capturing Almaligh. Algui retreated to the Tarim Basin where he remained a threat to Arigbokh. With this turn of events, Arigbokh lost his only significant supporter. [11]

Rebellion in China, 1262

In February, Li Dan rebelled at Yidu, and soon gained control of surrounding parts of Shandong. Khubilai's attention was diverted from the conflict with Arigbokh and was unable to benefit from Arigbokh's troubles with Algui. He sent Shi Tianzi and Shi Chu to suppress the rebellion. They defeated Li Dan at Jinan and captured him at Daming in August. [12]

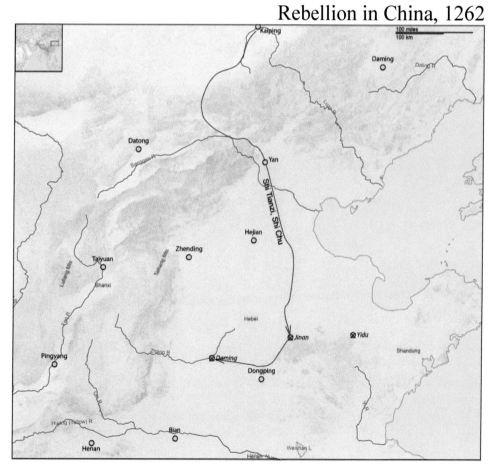

War between Berkh and Khulegu, 1262

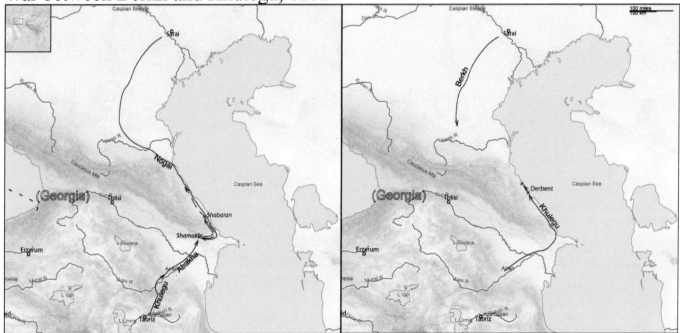

The sons of Zuchi had long claimed the area south of the Caucasus Mountains, based on the campaign of Zev and Subeedei in 1221. However, Khulegu had taken this area over during his campaigns. In 1262, Berkh moved to reclaim it, sending his nephew, Nogai, with his army past the Caucasus Mountains in August. Khulegu began moving north to confront him in September. Khulegu's advance force met Nogai at Shamakhi. Nogai defeated them but then retreated to Shabaran where he was defeated on November 14. Khulegu's main force caught up and continued to pursue north, taking Derbent on December 8 and defeating Nogai again further north on the 15th. [13]

War between Berkh and Khulegu, 1263

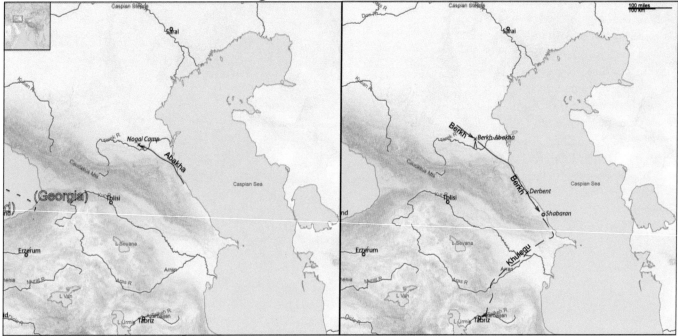

Khulegu's son, Abakha, pursued Nogai and his army, continuing the pursuit across the Terek River where he plundered Nogai's camp. At this point, Berkh arrived with his main army. In the battle fought on January 13, Abakha was forced to withdraw. While recrossing the Terek River, the ice gave way, resulting the further losses to his army. Abakha continued to retreat south to Shabaran. Berkh followed to Derbent and then returned home. Khulegu was still in the field with his main army but after Berkh withdrew, he and Abakha went back to Tabriz. [14]

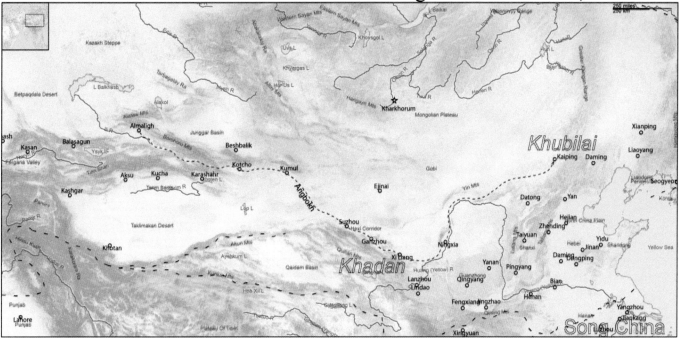

Arigbokh's forces continued to skirmish with Khubilai's during 1263, but by the following year, and after a severe winter in the steppe, Arigbokh realized that he was alone. He traveled to Kaiping where he surrendered to Khubilai. [15]

The Regional Khanates, 1264

The principal result of these Mongol civil wars was the transformation of the regions into independent countries which went their own way and frequently warred with one another. This transformation is shown by new names on the maps. The domains of Berkh and Khungiran are labeled the Golden Horde and White Horde. Algui's domain is labeled Tsagadai Khanate. The title of Great Khan is now held by Khubilai but it is a formality. His domain is labeled China which he ruled from a Chinese city as a Chinese Emperor. Khulegu acknowledged the sovereignty of Khubilai by taking the title of Il Khan, but he was independent for all practical purposes. His domain is labeled Ilkhanate. [16]

War between the Golden Horde and Byzantium, 1265

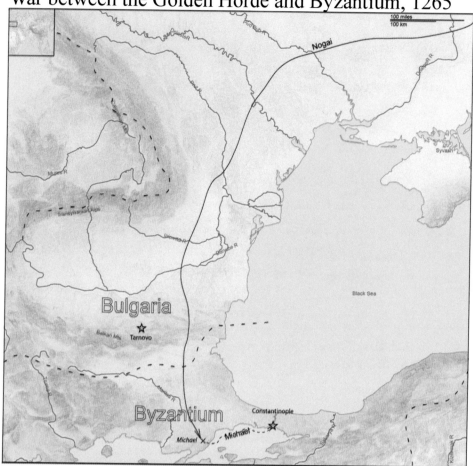

To further his conflict with the Ilkhanate, Berkh had made an alliance with Egypt. When envoys from Egypt were detained by the new Byzantine Emperor in Constantinople, Michael Paleologus, Berkh sent Nogai in spring 1265 to secure their release. Nogai marched through Bulgaria and defeated the Byzantines. Michael Paleologus barely escaped with his life and allowed the envoys to proceed. [17]

War between the Golden Horde and the Ilkhanate, 1265

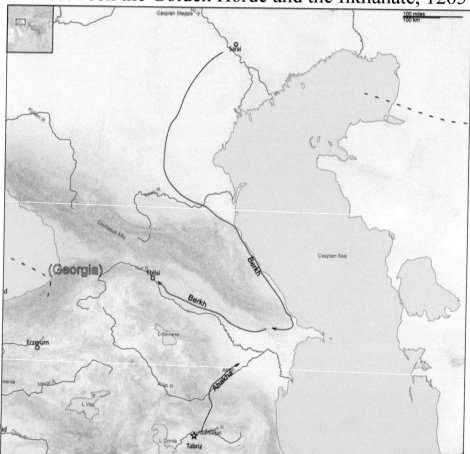

In summer 1265, Berkh led his army around the Caucasus Mountains as before. When Abakha, who had recently succeeded his father, moved north to confront him, Berkh turned west and moved up the Kur River Valley. Abakha followed him upriver. No battles occurred, however, because shortly after reaching Tblisi, Berkh died. His army returned home and Abakha made no move against them. [18]

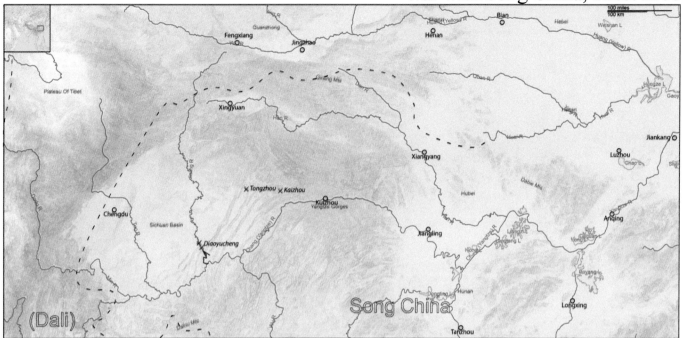

Khubilai was now free to resume the war with Song China. He sent a force to attack Diaoyucheng again. Song forces came up the river to meet the Mongols. The result was a Mongol victory in which they captured 146 ships. The Mongols also attacked Tongzhou. In 1266, the Mongols attacked Kaizhou. [19]

The Tsagadai Khanate, 1266

When Arigbokh surrendered, Algui regained control of the Tsagadai Khanate. However, he died shortly thereafter. Urgana, who had married Algui despite his takeover of her domain, had her now grown son, Mubarak Shah, enthroned in March. Khubilai, however, decided to appoint his own nominee, and sent Barak to take over in September. During the conflict between Barak and Mubarak Shah, Khaidu, a grandson of Ogedei, seized Almaligh for himself. [20]

War with Song China, 1267/1268

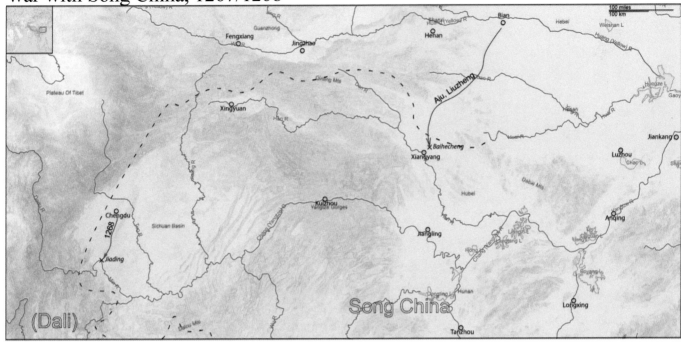

Khubilai continued to probe Song defenses, trying to find a weak point. In 1267 he dispatched Aju and Liu Zheng with a major army to Xiangyang. They arrived in October 1268. The Mongols also attacked Jiading in 1268. [21]

Khaidu, 1268/1269

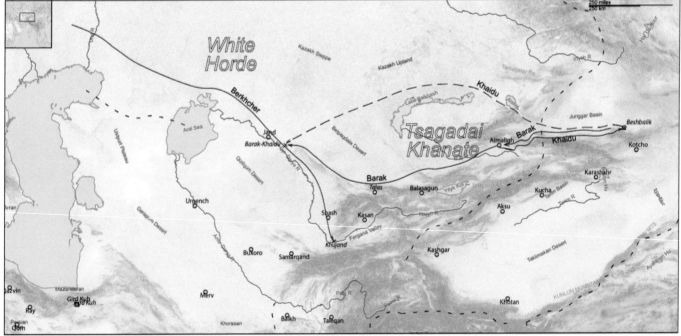

Khaidu attacked Beshbalik but was repulsed and fled to the west. Barak consolidated his power in the Tsagadai Khanate, recovered Almaligh, then pursued Khaidu. He defeated Khaidu on the Syr Darya River. Khaidu appealed to the Golden Horde for help and Monkhtomor sent his uncle Berkecher who defeated Barak at Khujand. A few months later, in 1269, Khaidu made peace with Barak and they both met with Berkecher at Talas to make peace with the Golden Horde and White Horde. [22]

In February, Khubilai sent Shi Tianzi to inspect the situation at Xiangyang. Xiangyang, and its twin city Fancheng, controlled the passage of the Han River at a key point. Both cities were fortified by double walls and connected by a pontoon bridge across the river. They had also laid in vast quantities of supplies to prepare for a long siege. Shi Tianzi recommended building a connected ring of forts around the twin cities and to tighten the siege. He also urged reinforcements and the use of riverboats. [23]

Siege of Xiangyang, 1269

Siege of Xiangyang, Summer 1269 to Fall 1272

Arigkhaya arrived with reinforcements and Liu Zheng constructed a fleet of riverboats. Song forces made repeated attempts to break out from the fortresses or to come to their relief: August 1269, March 1270, October 1270, August 1271, June 1272, and September 1272. This last attempt broke through to reach the cities but was then trapped inside. [24]

War with Song China, Summer 1269 to Fall 1272

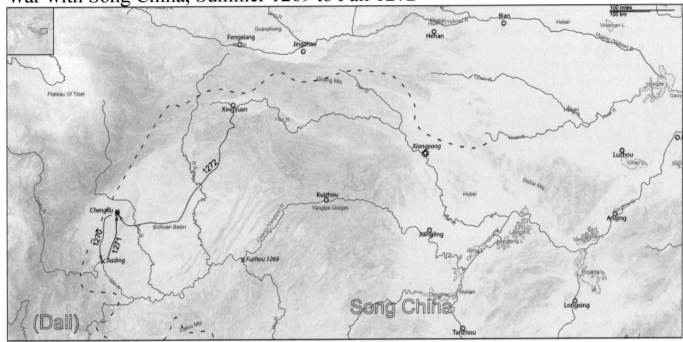

Sichuan was not ignored during the Mongol siege of Xiangyang. In 1269, Mongols attacked the area around Fuzhou. In 1270, they attacked Jiading again. In 1271, Song forces recovered Chengdu. The Mongols retook Chengdu in 1272. [25]

War between the Tsagadai Khanate and the Ilkhanate, 1270 to 1271

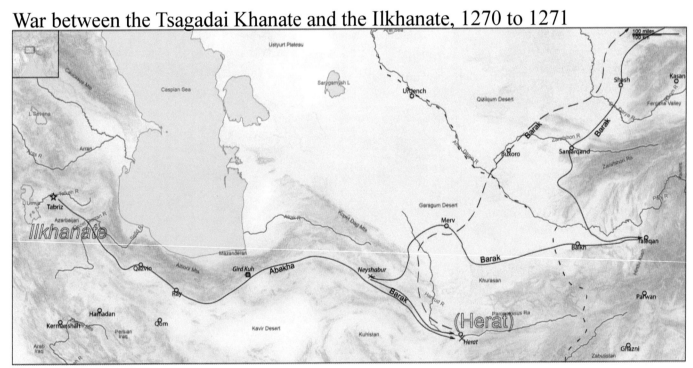

In the spring of 1270, Barak invaded Persia. At the same time, he instigated Teguder in Georgia to revolt against Abakha. Teguder was quickly defeated and Abakha marched to the east in April. Barak advanced to Neyshabur which he attacked on May 19. As Abakha advanced, Barak moved back to Herat. By July, Abakha reached Herat and defeated Barak in battle on July 22. Barak retreated and Abakha returned to Azerbaijan. Khaidu then moved against Barak, but Barak died in August 1271 and his son, Duva, along with his army, submitted to Khaidu. From this point on, Khaidu controlled the Tsagadai Khanate. The last Ismaili fortress, Gird Kuh, finally surrendered to the Mongols in 1271. [26]

After years of preparation, the Korean court finally returned from Ganghwa Island to Gaegyeong in 1270. A faction of the military, the Sambyeolcho, would not accept this, however, and revolted in June. They fled to Jindo and from there they gained control of three districts in the southwest. In May 1271, a combined Korean-Mongol force defeated them on Jindo. They fled further to Jejudo and held out there until April 1273 when they were finally defeated. [27]

Conflict in Central Asia, 1271 to 1273

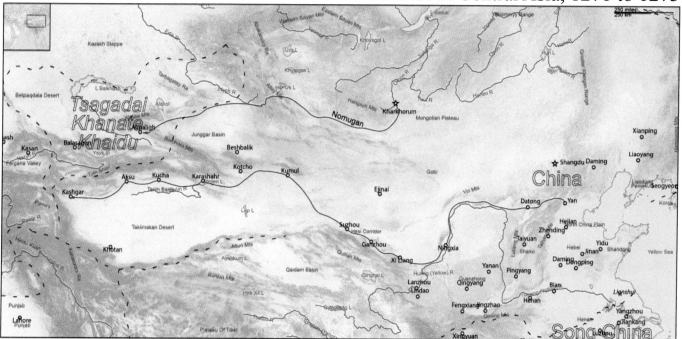

In 1266, Khubilai had appointed his son, Nomugan, as Prince of Pacification of the North, and stationed him at Kharkhorum. With Khaidu in control of the Tsagadai Khanate, Khubilai ordered Nomugan to that area to guard against incursions. Nomugan occupied Almaligh. Khubilai also sent supporting forces to occupy the cities of the Tarim Basin. Also, in 1271, Khubilai finished building his new capital, Dadu, beside the former Jin capital of Zhongdu. The court and administration moved to Dadu, but Kaiping, now known as Shangdu, would remain as the summer capital. [28]

Siege of Xiangyang, Winter 1272/1273

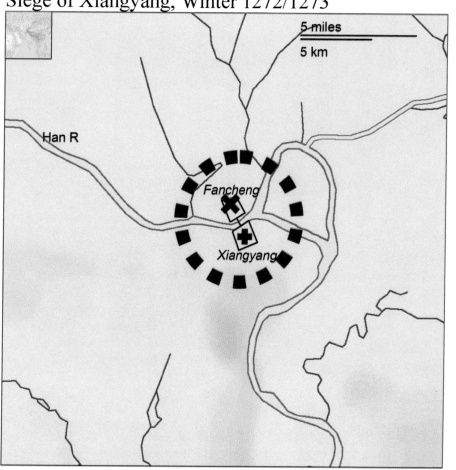

With Xiangyang still holding out, Khubilai had sent for Muslim engineers from Persia to construct advanced counterweight trebuchets. These had a longer range and greater accuracy than the torsion trebuchets used up to this point. By December they were finally ready. Within a short time, they had breached the walls of Fancheng and Mongol troops stormed into the city. All the defenders were killed. Seeing this, and seeing the new trebuchets being moved across the river, the Song commander at Xiangyang, Lu Wenhuan, was induced to surrender. This occurred on March 17. The fall of Xiangyang did not immediately clear the way. There was another twin fortress further down river, and strong Song forces were in place where the Han River met up with the Chang (Yangtze) River. [29]

Expedition to Japan, Fall 1274

Khubilai had been sending envoys to Japan ordering submission since 1266 but all were rejected or ignored. In 1274, he organized a combined Mongol-Korean force, similar, if slightly larger, than the one that had successfully taken Jejudo the previous year. This expedition sailed for Japan on October 3. They captured Tsushima on October 5. Moving on they took Iki on October 14, Hirado on the 16th, and Nokono, in Hakata Bay, two weeks later. After landing at Hakata they were confronted by local Japanese forces and fought two battles. The Japanese had some success but were forced to retreat to Dazaifu, the local fortress. However, the Mongols, having limited resources, decided to withdraw. Due to losses in battle, and storm damage along the way back, only two thirds of the force returned to Korea safely in late November. [30]

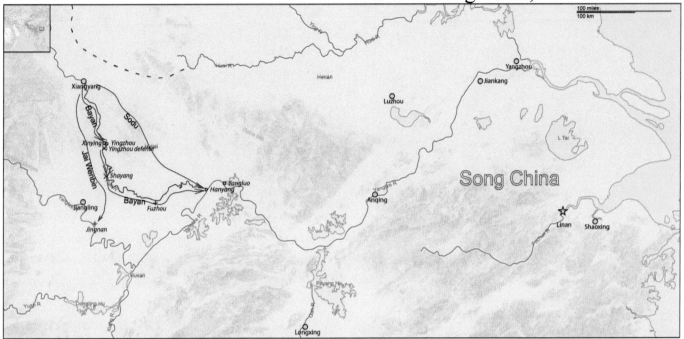

Bayan, assisted by Aju and Arigkhaya, took command of a reinforced and reorganized army and began to move south from Xiangyang in October. When they reached the twin fortresses of Yingzhou and Xinying, Bayan chose not to get tied down in a lengthy siege. Instead, he dragged his riverboats overland to a stream that ran west of the cities and flowed into the Han River further down. When the defenders of Yingzhou tried to pursue, he defeated them in the field. The Mongols took Shayang on November 22. Fuzhou surrendered on December 13. Eleven days later, the army arrived in front of Hanyang. [31]

War with Song China, Winter 1275

Bayan outmaneuvered the Song commander, Xia Gui, occupied Shawukou on January 7, and got his ships into the Chang (Yangtze) River. Bayan next attacked the Yangluo fortress and directed Aju to cross the river. On January 11, Aju seized Qingshanji on the southern bank and Mongol ships defeated the Song navy. Yangluo fell on January 12. Both Hanyang and Ezhou surrendered on January 16. Bayan proceeded down the Chang. Cities surrendered as the Mongols approached. Bayan reached Anqing on February 27, and met up with Atakhai. Jia Sidao, the Song prime minister, assembled a large army, met Xia Gui who had fled from Shawukou, and prepared to meet the Mongol advance. [32]

War with Song China, Spring 1275

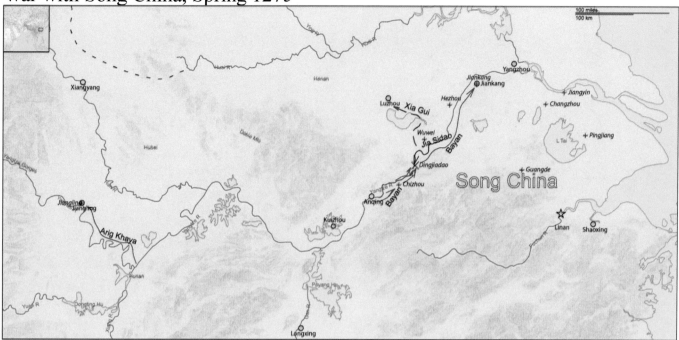

Jia Sidao and Xia Gui proceeded upstream to Dingjiadao. As they did so, Bayan moved downstream, reaching Chizhou, which surrendered on March 4. On March 17, he left Chizhou and battled Jia Sidao at Dingjiadao two days later. The Song forces collapsed at the first Mongol assault, which came on the river and both banks. Jia Sidao and Xia Gui both fled the scene. Following this loss, many Song cities in the area surrendered as Bayan moved down the Chang (Yangtze) River. The surrender of Jiankang, the largest city on the lower Chang River, on March 30 was particularly important. On the upper Chang, Arigkhaya advanced to take Jiangling. [33]

Conflict in Central Asia, 1275

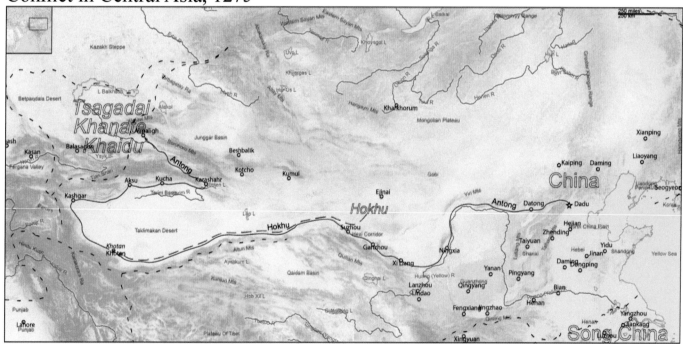

During the war with Song China, Hokhu, a son of Guyug, rebelled at Emil. Khubilai sent Antong with an army to the west. Antong defeated Hokhu, who then fled to Khotan. Antong then went on to reinforce Nomugan at Almaligh. [34]

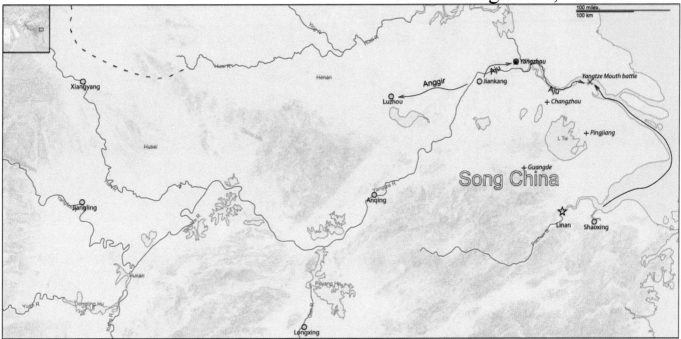

Bayan was recalled to the capital for consultation in May but Aju continued to consolidate Mongol gains. He moved to take Yangzhou which put up a strong defense. Xia Gui, who had retreated to Luzhou, was neutralized by Anggir but still held out. One final effort was made by a Song fleet of ocean going ships which sailed into the Chang (Yangtze) River. Some of the Song cities that had surrendered went back to Song allegiance. Aju defeated the fleet and the cities surrendered to the Mongols again. [35]

War with Song China, Fall/Winter, 1275/1276

On November 27 at Jiankang, Bayan set three columns in motion towards Linan, the Song capital. With himself and Atakhai, commanding the center, he moved east of Lake Tai. Alakhan, commanding the right wing, advanced to the west of Lake Tai. The left wing, a naval force led by Dong Wenping, sailed down river and followed the coast. Bayan encountered resistance at Changzhou which was quickly defeated. With no further opposition he arrived at Linan February 1. Alakhan and Dong Wenping arrived February 5. A few days were spent negotiating the terms of surrender and on February 10, Bayan entered Linan in triumph. However, two young Song princes had escaped by sea to the south. [36]

War with Song China, Spring to Winter 1276

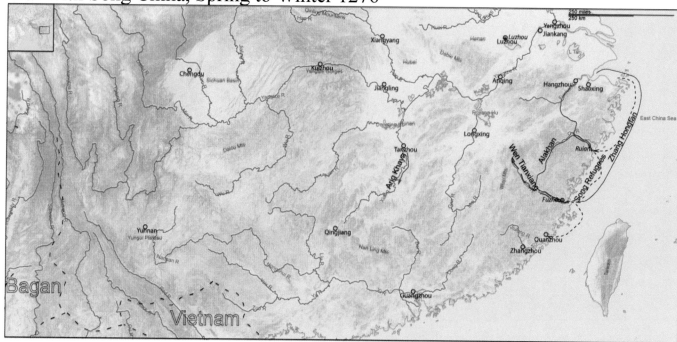

The Song refugees, fleeing by sea with the two young princes, stopped briefly at Ruian, and then moved on to Fuzhou. There, on June 14, they enthroned the oldest boy as the new Song emperor. However, Mongol armies and fleets were already in pursuit. As they moved closer to Fuzhou, some of the refugees fled by sea with the new Emperor to Quanzhou. Others followed Wen Tianxiang inland. Fuzhou surrendered in December. Xia Gui had surrendered at Luzhou in March. Arigkhaya had captured Tanzhou in January. In July, he began to move further south. [37]

Conflict in Central Asia, 1276/1277

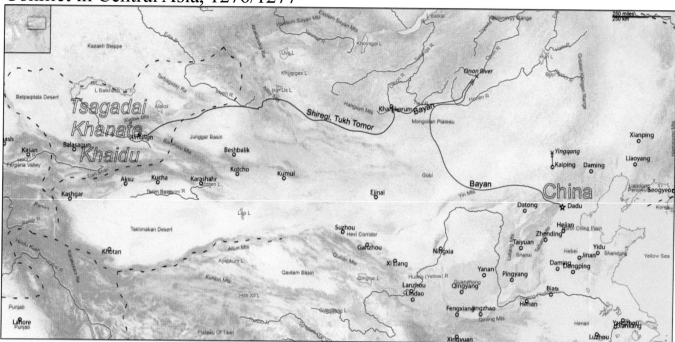

In September 1276, Shirigi and Tukhtomor, princes serving under Nomugan, mutinied with their forces and captured both Nomugan and Antong. They turned their prisoners over to Khaidu who sent Nomugan on to the Golden Horde. As a result, Khaidu recovered Almaligh. Shirigi and Tukhtomor went on to seize Kharkhorum itself in 1277. Jirwadai at Yingqang also revolted. Bayan was sent to restore order. He defeated Shirigi and Tukhtomor on the Orhon River in August and recovered Kharkhorum. Jirwadai was defeated by Bai Tomor. Khaidu's position was strengthened and he remained a threat to Khubilai. Nomugan would remain a prisoner of the Golden Horde for ten years. [38]

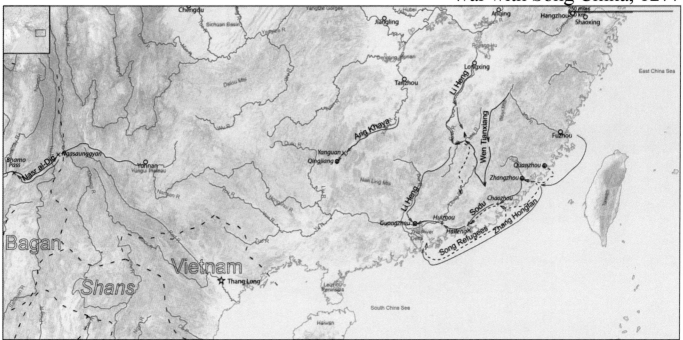

The Song refugees kept moving until they reached the Zhu River Delta where they could hide among the many islands. The Mongol fleet was always close behind. Further inland, Wen Tianxiang managed to raise an army and counterattacked. Li Heng came south with a Mongol army and defeated him. Arigkhaya continued to move south as well. He defeated local forces at Yanguan and occupied Qingjiang. Guangzhou was occupied by Li Heng in November. In the far southwest, Khubilai had made the vassal kingdom of Dali into a regular province in 1273, causing border conflicts and an incursion from Bagan. The incursion was defeated at Ngasaunggyan. Mongol forces advanced to the Bhamo Pass. [39]

War with Egypt, 1277

The Egyptian Sultan, Baibars, invaded Anatolia in 1277 and defeated a Seljuk/Mongol force at Elbistan on April 15. Baibars then occupied Kayseri. Abakha moved to counter this invasion, but Baibars retreated to Syria and Abakha did not pursue. Baibars died at Dimashq (Damascus) on July 1. [40]

War with Song China, 1278/1279

The Song refugees fled further to the Leizhou Peninsula and considered moving even further south to Champa, but turned back and fortified themselves at Yaishan. Wen Tianxiang was captured at Xunzhou in February 1279. Li Heng and Zhang Hongfan moved against Yaishan in March 1279 and broke through the line of Song ships. The last Song emperor died March 19, when his Prime Minister held him and jumped into the sea. The last Song holdouts in Sichuan were also captured, Chongqing and Kuizhou in 1278, and Diaoyucheng in February 1279. [41]

Wars and Expeditions, 1280 to 1304

Countries & Peoples – 1/1/1280

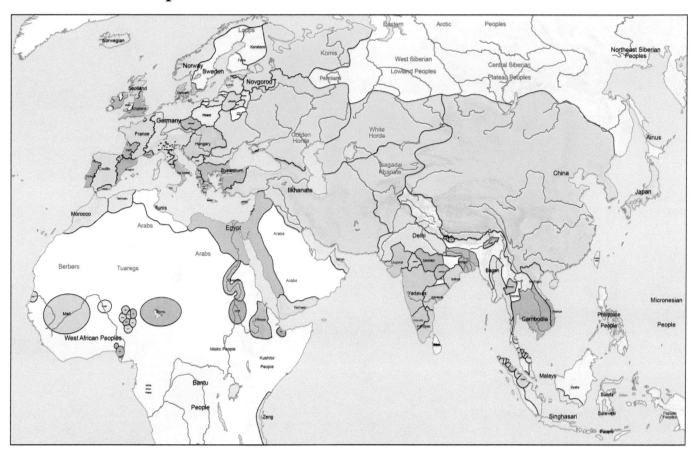

Some principal events between 1260 and 1280.

Africa. Bornu merged with Kanem 1260.

Western Europe. New: Papacy, Two Sicilies 1266.

Eastern Europe. New: Lithuania 1263.

Middle East. Mongolia-Halab (Aleppo) war 1260. Mongolia-Egypt war 1260. Golden Horde-Ilkhanate war 1262-1265. Tsagadai-Ilkhanate war 1270-1271. Egypt-Ilkhanate war 1277.

Central Asia. Arigbokh and Khubilai both claimed status of Great Khan 1260. Arigbokh-Khubilai war 1260-1264. Unity of the Mongol Empire lost 1264. China-Tsagadai intermittent war 1271-1304.

Eastern Asia. Mongolia-Song China war 1260-1261, 1265-1279. Mongolia-Japan war 1274

Southern Asia. No significant events.

South-Eastern Asia. Singhasari conquered Srivijaya and Malayu 1275.

The Mongol Khanates, 1280

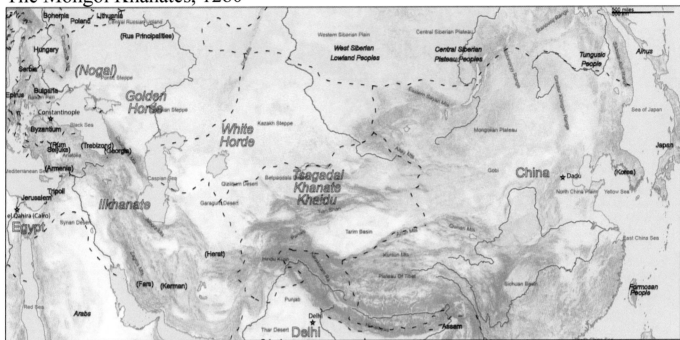

Song China was the last of the great conquests. The Mongol Empire had split up and already begun to lose ground in the west. With the empire no longer unified, none of its parts were able mount an offensive that would have been strong enough to advance further. Future campaigns and expeditions would be limited in nature, frequently met with failure, and often against other Mongols.

War with Egypt, 1280/1281

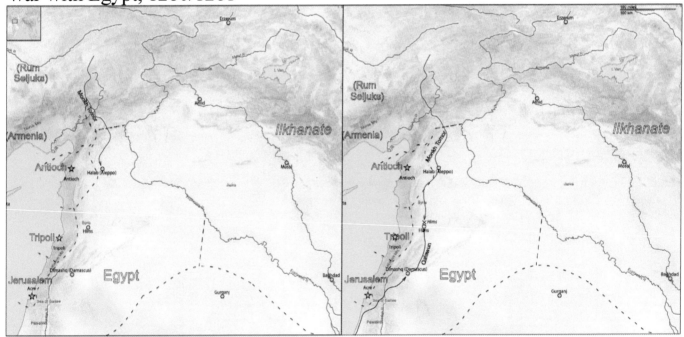

In the summer of 1280, the Il-Khan, Abakha, sent his brother, Monkhtomor, into Syria. More of a raid than an invasion, the army reached Halab (Aleppo) and then withdrew. Anticipating another invasion, the new Egyptian Sultan, Qalawun, left El Qahira (Cairo) in April the following year. He reached Dimashq (Damascus) in May. The anticipated invasion came in September with a larger army, again led by Monkhtomor. The Mongols passed Halab in October. Qalawun, moved north from Dimashq and the armies met north of Hims. The Mongols were defeated and withdrew. [1]

Khubilai had sent more embassies to Japan but in 1275 and 1279, the ambassadors were executed. After the defeat of the last Song loyalists, Khubilai planned a second expedition. An eastern army left Korea on May 2. It took Tsushima and Iki again, raided Shikanoshima, and then settled at Hirado to wait for the southern army. The much larger southern army, assembling in eastern China, encountered many delays, but finally arrived at Hirado in late June. The combined force then sailed to Hakata Bay. Since the first expedition, the Japanese had fortified the shoreline of the bay and the Mongol forces could not make a secure landing. Skirmishing continued throughout July and early August until August 15, when the area was struck by a typhoon. Most of the Mongol fleet was destroyed and only part of the army was able to return to Korea. [2]

Expedition to Japan, 1281

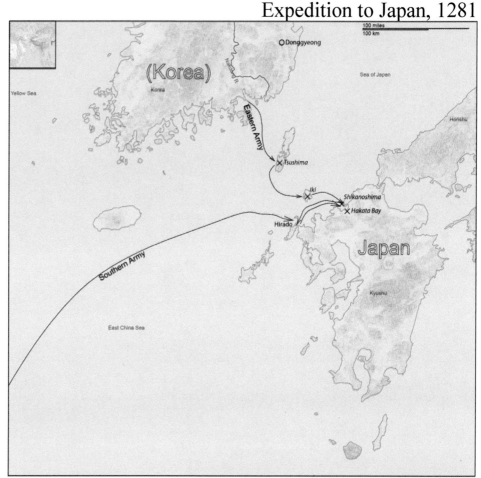

Expedition to Champa, 1281/1282

Champa had responded to Khubilai's embassies by sending tribute and professing submission. However, the ruler of Champa, Indravarman, did not come in person as Khubilai had demanded. In 1281, Sodu sailed from Guangzhou to enforce this demand. His army easily captured Vijaya, but Indravarman retreated into the mountainous interior and would not give battle. Mongol reinforcements under Atakhai arrived in 1282 but they still could not capture Indravarman. [3]

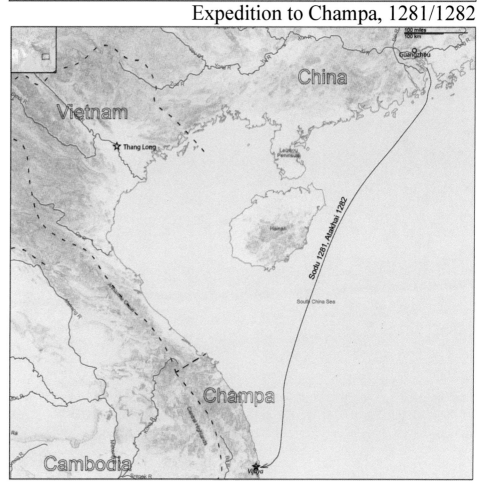

War with Bagan, 1283 to 1285

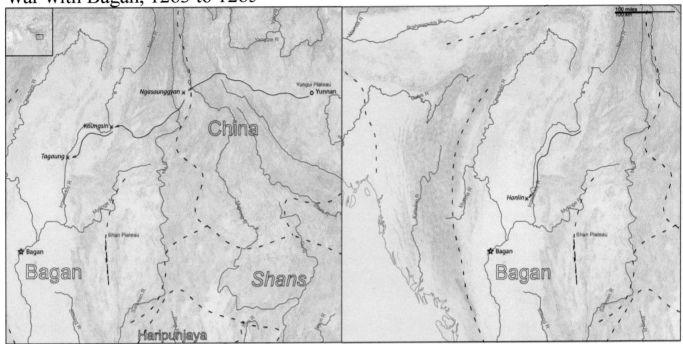

Continuing raids across the border from Bagan, led to another Mongol invasion in 1283. The ruler of Bagan, Narathihapate fled to the south. In 1285, the Mongols advanced further south but did not reach Bagan itself. [4]

War in Central Asia, 1284 to 1286

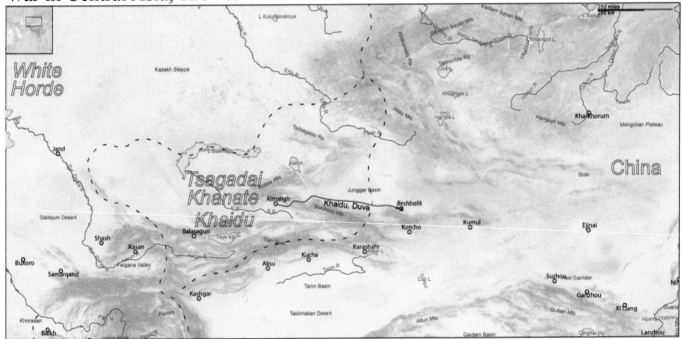

Khaidu had some difficulty controlling the Tsagadai Khanate through puppet Khans. The first one he appointed soon developed a desire for independence and had to be deposed. Some of the sons of Algui and Barak also resisted Khaidu's control. Finally, in 1282, he appointed Duva as Khan. They formed a lasting partnership which would hold until Khaidu's death. Khaidu and Duva attacked Beshbalik and captured it in 1286. [5]

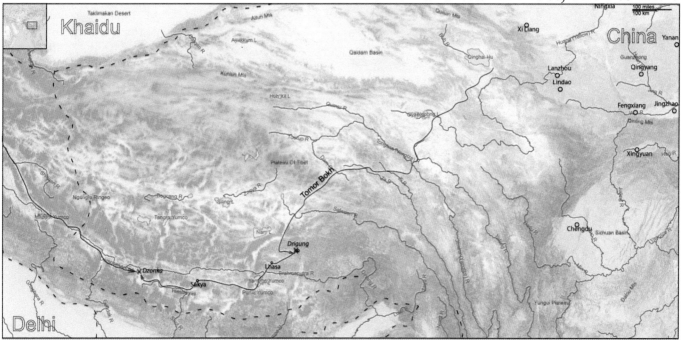

Mongol rule in Tibet was centered on the Sakya monastery. In 1284, the area around the Drigung monastery revolted. In 1290 Khubilai sent his grandson, Bokhtomor, who defeated the rebellion. Khaidu attempted to intervene and sent a force into Tibet. Bokhtomor defeated this force at Dzonka. [6]

War with Delhi, 1285/1287

In the 1250's. Bat had sent forces to join in Khulegu's invasion of the west. During the war between Berkh and Khulegu in the 1260's, these troops broke away and established themselves in eastern Persia where they maintained an independent existence south of the Hindu Kush mountains. They became known as Neguderis, after their early commander, Neguder. In the 1280's they began to mount raids into India. In February 1285, Tomor invaded the territory of Delhi. He defeated and killed Muhammad Khan, crown prince of Delhi, near Multan. In early 1287, Tomor invaded again and ravaged the area between Lahore and Samana. [7]

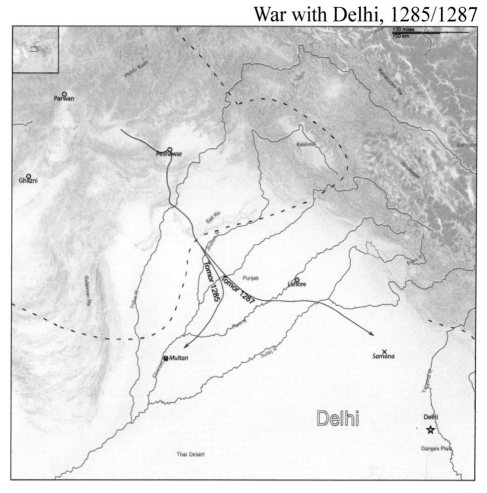

War with Hungary, Winter/Spring 1285/1286

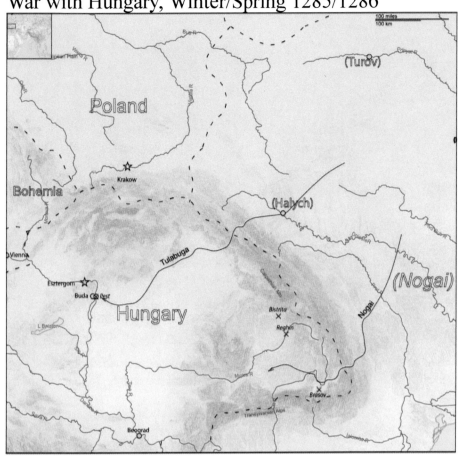

The Golden Horde had not abandoned its claim to Hungary but had never enforced it. In the winter of 1285, Nogai decided to do just that. The Golden Horde Khan, Tulabuga, led the main army. Crossing the Carpathian Mountains, they suffered losses in the heavy snow. Tulabuga's reduced army reached and burned Pest but did not cross the Danube River. Tulabuga raided the countryside but was unable to take castles. When confronted by a Hungarian army he was defeated. Nogai's army invaded from the south and also raided the countryside but he too could not take castles. After a defeat by local forces, Nogai withdrew when the main Hungarian army approached. [8]

War with Champa and Vietnam, 1285/1286

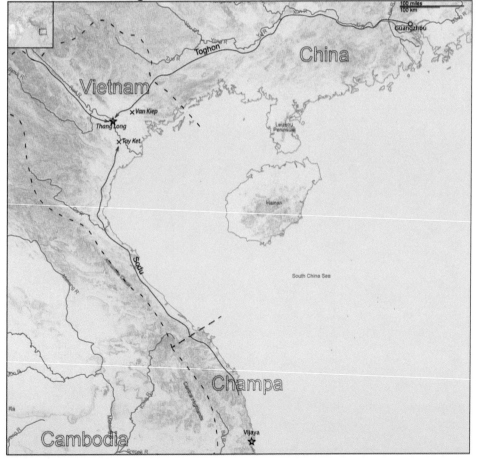

The war with Champa became a war with Vietnam when Vietnam's ruler, Tran Nhan Tong, refused to allow Mongol passage to Champa through his territory. Three Mongol armies advanced, one overland from Guangzhou under Toghon, one from Dali, and Sodu was ordered to attack Vietnam from the south. Once again Thang Long was quickly occupied, but Tran Nhan Tong had left the capital and organized resistance in the countryside. Sodu's army was attacked and defeated at Tay Ket, and Sodu was killed. Toghon's forces were defeated at Van Kiep but Toghon managed to save his army and withdraw to China. [9]

War with Bagan, 1287

Narathihapate had not found refuge in the south and decided to submit to the Mongols. After some negotiation, he signed a treaty and sent an embassy of submission in 1286. When he was retuning to Bagan in 1287, he was poisoned by one of his sons who renounced the treaty. The country descended into anarchy and Khubilai sent his grandson, Esentomor, to restore order. Esentomor marched on Bagan. After fighting at Myinsaing, he withdrew. The Mongols created a nominal province of Mianzhong but it did not control anything. [10]

Rebellion in the Northeast, 1287 to 1289

Nayan revolted against Khubilai in May, with support from other princes in the northeast and local tribes. Khubilai himself led an army to deal with this. He also dispatched Bayan to Kharkhorum to prevent Khaidu from intervening. Nayan was defeated on July 14 and captured a short time later. He was executed. Another prince, Shikhtur, was also defeated. It was not until 1289, however, that all the rebel forces were suppressed. [11]

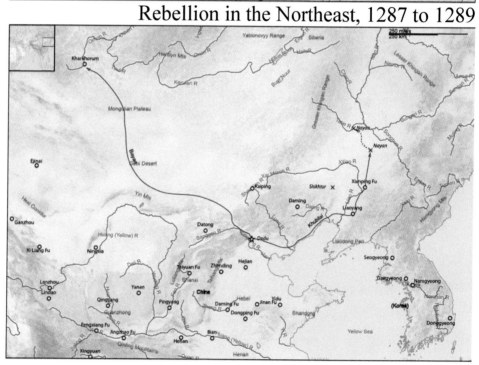

War with Vietnam, 1287/1288

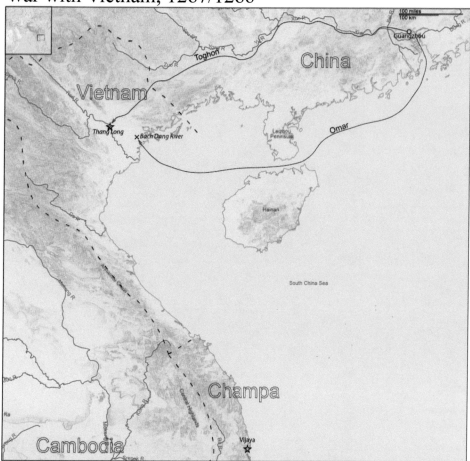

Khubilai sent Toghon back to Vietnam in 1287, this time with support from the sea. Once again, the Mongols occupied the capital but were harassed in the countryside. The Mongol fleet was trapped in the Bach Dang River and destroyed. Toghon withdrew again. [12]

War with Poland, Winter/Spring 1287/1288

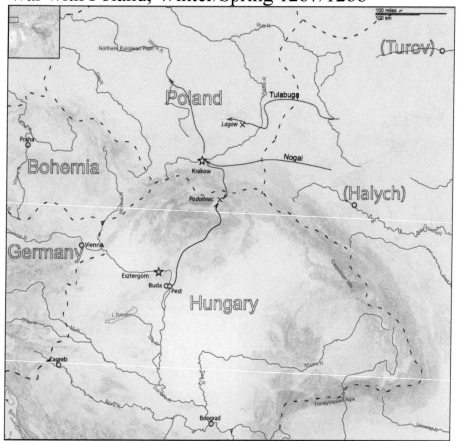

Nogai and Tulabuga next invaded Poland. Tulabuga led the north column. He was defeated at Lagow but moved on for a short way before withdrawing. Nogai and the south column advanced to Krakow. Unable to take the city, Nogai sent detachments to raid north and south. An army from Hungary came up to defeat the southern detachment at Podolinec. Nogai then withdrew as well. [13]

War between the Golden Horde and the Ilkhanate, 1288/1290

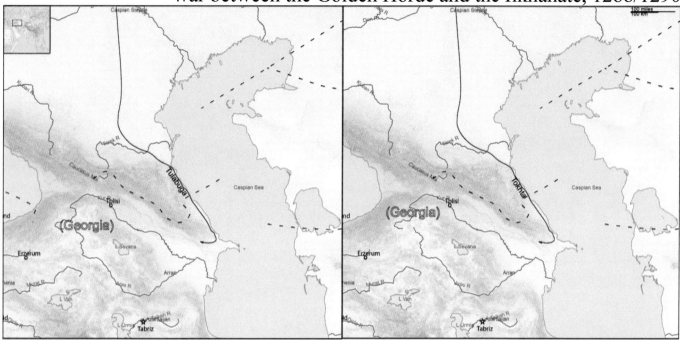

In the spring of 1288, Tulabuga invaded south of the Caucasus. The Il-Khan, Argun, advanced to meet him and defeated him. In the spring of 1290, the new Golden Horde Khan, Tokhta, invaded. Argun advanced to meet him and defeated him as well. [14]

War in Central Asia, 1289/1290

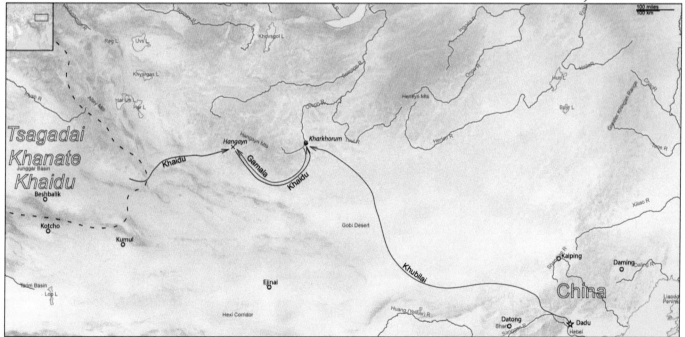

Khubilai's grandson, Gamala, had been commanding at Kharkhorum since 1286. In 1289, he moved against Khaidu. Khaidu defeated him in the Hangay Mountains and went on to take Kharkhorum. Khubilai himself then marched on Kharkhorum the following year, but there was no confrontation since Khaidu retreated. By this time, continued raids by Khaidu's forces had caused Khubilai to abandon the cities in the Tarim Basin. [15]

War between the Tsagadai Khanate and the Ilkhanate, 1291

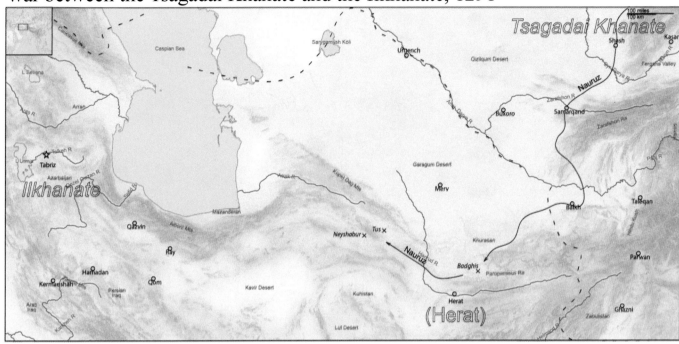

In 1289, Nauruz led a revolt in Khurasan against Argun. Argun defeated him but Nauruz sought refuge with Khaidu and Duva. In 1291, Argun died and there was a struggle for succession in the Ilkhanate. Khaidu's forces invaded Persia with Nauruz leading the advance. Nauruz remained in control of Khurasan for a year. [16]

War with Delhi, 1291/1292

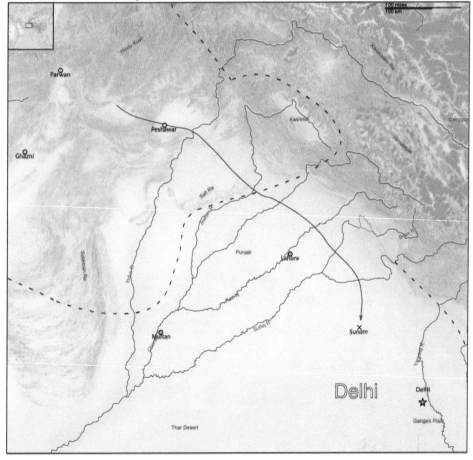

In 1291, Delhi Sultan Firuz marched against the Neguderis. The following year, the Neguderis retaliated and invaded as far as Sunam where Firuz defeated them. [17]

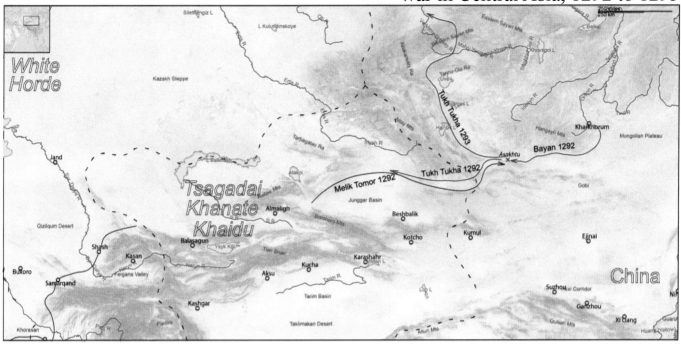

In the fall of 1292, Khaidu's army took the offensive again. Bayan, still in Mongolia, defeated Melik Tomor at the Akhsutu ridge. Tukh Tukha followed this up by crossing the Altai mountains and capturing 3,000 of Khaidu's troops. In 1293, Tukh Tukha drove Khaidu's forces out of the Yenisey valley. [18]

Expedition to Java, 1293

Kertanagara, ruler of Singhasari, had also rejected Khubilai's demand for submission and sent the Mongol envoys back with mutilated faces. In 1292, on Java, Panjalu and Madura had rebelled against Kertanagara and killed him. In 1293, not knowing this, a Mongol fleet and army, commanded by Shi Bi, sailed from Quanzhou to enforce submission. When the Mongols arrived at Tuban, Vijaya, Kertanagara's son-in-law, appealed to them for help. Panjalu was defeated at Kediri with Mongol help, but Vijaya then turned against the Mongols, lured them into an ambush, and defeated them at Majapahit. Shi Bi retreated to his ships and sailed back to China. [19]

War between the Tsagadai Khanate and the Ilkhanate, 1294/1295

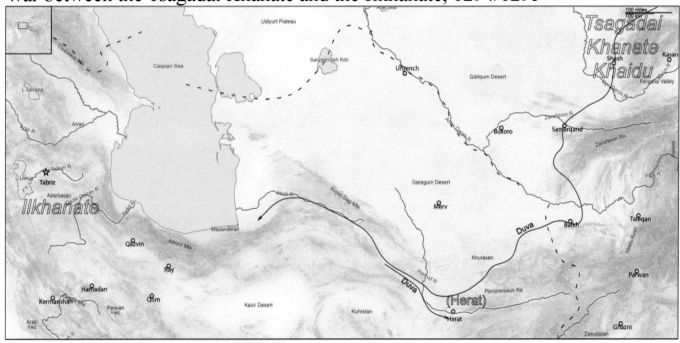

Gazan, a son of Argun, defeated Duva's forces in 1294 and Nauruz, surrendered to him. Duva then invaded Khurasan himself while Gazan was occupied in a civil war. Duva occupied Mazanderan for eight months. As he withdrew in 1295, Duva sent a force to Herat and attacked several cities in that area before returning north. [20]

War with Delhi, 1299

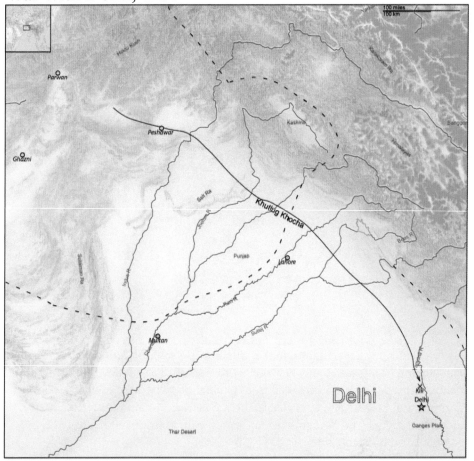

In the late 1290's, Khaidu and Duva gained control of the Neguderis. They appointed Duva's son, Khutlug Khocha, to rule over them. This led to a more serious effort and larger armies being sent against the Delhi Sultanate. In 1299, Khutlug Khocha led a Mongol army directly to Delhi. In a battle at Kili, the Mongol left wing was defeated by Zafar Khan but then Zafar Khan was ambushed, and his force destroyed. However, the Mongols withdrew because Khutlug Khocha had been wounded and soon died. [21]

In October 1299, Gazan, now Il-Khan, invaded Syria. Bypassing Halab (Aleppo), he was confronted by an Egyptian army at Wadi al-Khazandar and defeated it. The Syrian cities surrendered and Gazan advanced unopposed to Dimashq (Damascus). He sent some forces further south, raiding as far as Gaza. However, news of an incursion from the Tsagadai Khanate caused Gazan to withdraw. [22]

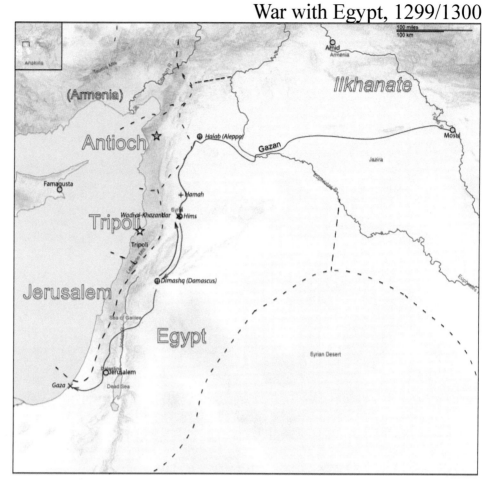

War between the Tsagadai Khanate and the Ilkhanate, 1300-1302

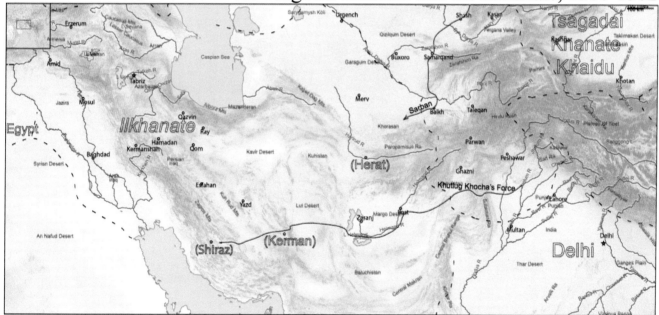

As Khutlug Khocha's forces returned from their invasion of India in 1300, they raided into Kerman and Shiraz. In 1302, Khaidu's son, Sarban, invaded Khurasan but encountered bad weather which prevented him from cooperating with Khutlug Khocha's force. Gazan's son, Oljiit, was able to block the invasion. [23]

War in Central Asia, 1300/1301

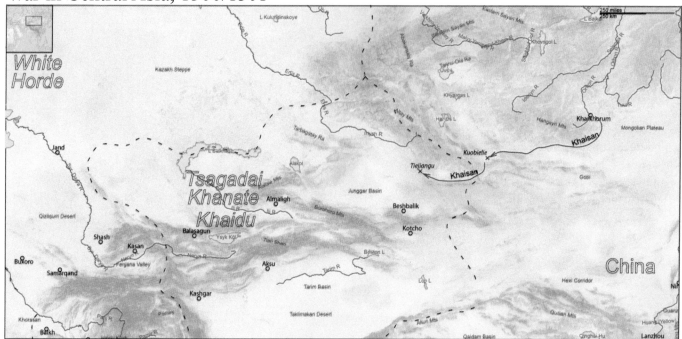

Khubilai had died in 1294 and his grandson, Tomor, succeeded him. Tomor paid more attention to his northern borders. In 1300, Tomor ordered a major campaign against Khaidu. Khaisan led a large army which initially defeated Khaidu at Kuobielie. Khaidu retreated to Mount Tiejiangu where they fought another battle on September 3. This was a major victory for Khaisan. However, Khaidu recovered and fought two more battles in the area which were inconclusive. Both armies returned to their bases. The conflict ended when Khaidu died in 1301. Duva would then assert himself as the sole ruler of the Tsagadai Khanate. [24]

War with Delhi, 1302

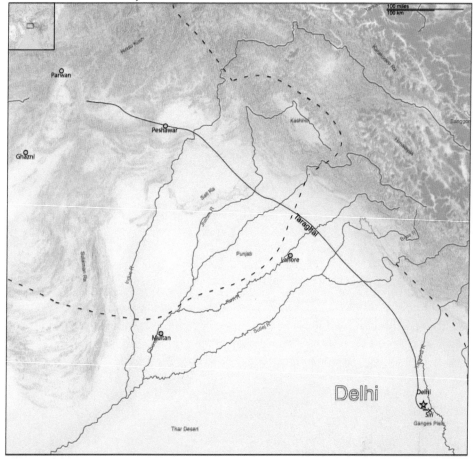

Taragai led another large Mongol army to Delhi in 1302, while most of Delhi's forces were engaged in the south. Delhi Sultan Ala ad-Din fortified himself at Siri which the Mongols besieged for two months. Siri held out and Taragai retreated as summer approached. [25]

Gazan returned to the war with Egypt in 1303. From Baghdad he marched up the west bank of the Euphrates River as far as Rahba but went no further. Another column, advancing from the north, had reached Dimashq (Damascus) but was defeated by local forces. [26]

Epilogue
Countries & Peoples – 1/1/1304

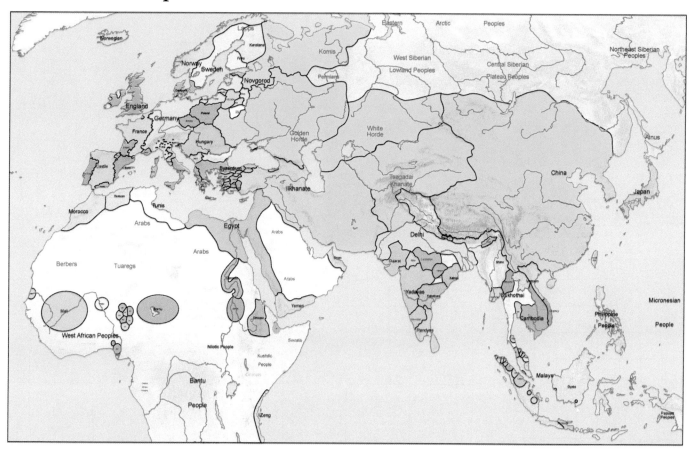

Some principal events between 1280 and 1304.

Africa. Ifat replaced Adal 1285.

Western Europe. Genoa took Corsica and Sardinia 1284. Aragon took Sicily 1282. England took Scotland 1296.

Eastern Europe. Golden Horde-Hungary war 1285-1286. Golden Horde-Poland war 1287-1288.

Middle East. New: multiple small countries in Anatolia from Byzantium 1291-1300. Egypt-Ilkhanate war 1281, 1299-1300, 1303.

Central Asia. China-Tsagadai intermittent war 1271-1304.

Eastern Asia. China-Japan war 1281.

Southern Asia. Tsagadai-Delhi war 1285, 1292, 1299, 1302. Delhi conquered Bengal 1287

South-Eastern Asia. New: Matarban from Bagan 1287, Lavo from Cambodia 1289. China-Champa war 1281-1282, 1285-1286. China-Vietnam war 1285-1286, 1287-1288. China-Bagan war 1283-1285, 1287, Bagan collapsed 1287. Sukhothai defeated Cambodia 1289. Majapahit overthrew Singhasari 1293.

In 1304 the Mongol Khanates made peace with one another. Trade and interchange of ideas could resume. However, plague outbreaks in southwestern China in the 1330's began to spread by the same way that had made those interchanges possible. By 1350, the plague had spread all the way to the Atlantic Ocean. Widespread death caused destabilization of states and societies everywhere. Il-Khan Persia fell into disarray in the 1330's. The Tsagadai Khanate began a process of subdivision in the 1340's. There was famine and widespread rebellion in China from the 1340's on, which would lead to the fall of the Mongol Yuan dynasty in 1368. Similar troubles engulfed the Golden Horde in the 1350's which weakened their hold on the Rus principalities. The Great Mongol Empire faded away but in its brief existence it had changed the world.

Chronological Index

As noted in the introduction, The romanization of foreign names is a difficult problem. Many countries have adopted new systems in recent years, but a lot of the sources used older systems. I have tried to conform to the most current usage as best I could. I apologize for any inadvertent errors.

Mongolian names are written according to modern Mongolian spelling, using Mongol Wikipedia and a recent Mongol translation of the *Secret History* as guides, converted from the Cyrillic alphabet. Alternate spellings are included in the Name and Subject Index in parentheses where the alternates are more common, eg Chinggis (Genghis).

Chinese names are written using the Pinyin system. Place names are the names used at the time. Corresponding modern names of major cities are shown in the Index.

Korean names are written using the Revised Romanization system. Place names are the names used at the time. Corresponding modern names of major cities are shown in the Index.

Place names in the west are written using their modern names except for Constantinople.

Events are generally listed in chronological order. Due to the lack of exact dates for most events, there may be some events slightly out of sequence. This is more of a problem when events occur in different areas where it was sometimes difficult to merges the sequences together.

145

Ao Dongxiang moved to relieve Xijing, 1212, 34

Migukou, Chinggis vs Ao Dongxiang, Mongol victory, 1212, 34

Chinggis wounded at Xijing, 1212, 34

Dexingzhou, taken by Mongols, 1212, 34

Chinggis advanced to Dexingzhou, 1213, 34

Dexingzhou, taken by Mongols, 1213, 34

Weiquan, Chinggis vs Wanyan Gang, Mongol victory, 1213, 34

Zev moved to outflank Juyongguan, 1213, October, 34

Feihuguan, taken by Mongols, 1213, 34

Zuqingguan, taken by Mongols, 1213, 34

Chinggis moved to Wuhuiling, 1213, 35

Zhuhu Gaoqi moved to confront Chinggis at Wuhuiling, 1213, 35

Wuhuiling, Chinggis vs Zhuhu Gaoqi, Mongol victory, 1213, 35

Zev advanced to Juyongguan from the south, 1213, 35

Juyongguan, taken by Mongols, 1213, 35

Yizhou, taken by Mongols, 1213, 35

Chinggis camped at Longhutai, 1213, 35

Zhuozhou, taken by Mongols, 1213, November, 35

Chinggis began invasion of Jin China, 1213, 35

Baozhou, taken by Mongols, 1213, 35

Bazhou, taken by Mongols, 1213, 35

Jizhou, taken by Mongols, 1213, 35

Xidinghu, taken by Mongols, 1213, 35

Hejian, taken by Mongols, 1213, 35

Luanzhou, taken by Mongols, 1213, 35

Qingzhou, resisted the Mongols, 1213, 35

Cangzhou, taken by Mongols, 1213, 35

Pingzhou, taken by Mongols, 1213, 35

Shenzhou, taken by Mongols, 1213, 35

Zhending, resisted the Mongols, 1213, 35

Dezhou, taken by Mongols, 1213, 35

Dizhou, taken by Mongols, 1213, 35

Enzhou, taken by Mongols, 1213, 35

Xingzhou, taken by Mongols, 1213, 35

Bozhou, taken by Mongols, 1213, 35

Daming, resisted the Mongols, 1213, 35

Yidu, taken by Mongols, 1213, 35

Jinan, taken by Mongols, 1213, 35

Mingzhou, taken by Mongols, 1213, 35

Weizhou, taken by Mongols, 1213, 35

Cizhou, taken by Mongols, 1213, 35

Laizhou, taken by Mongols, 1213, 35

Taian, taken by Mongols, 1213, 35

Dengzhou, taken by Mongols, 1213, 35

Dongping, resisted the Mongols, 1213, 35

Zhangde, taken by Mongols, 1213, 35

Luan, taken by Mongols, 1213, 35

Mizhou, taken by Mongols, 1214, 35

Pingyang, taken by Mongols, 1214, 35

Xizhou, taken by Mongols, 1214, 35

Haizhou, resisted the Mongols, 1214, 35

Jizhou, taken by Mongols, 1214, 35

Beizhou, resisted the Mongols, 1214, 35

Fenzhou, taken by Mongols, 1214, 35

Xizhou, taken by Mongols, 1214, 35

Xuzhou, resisted the Mongols, 1214, 35

Lanxian, taken by Mongols, 1214, 35

Taiyuan, taken by Mongols, 1214, 35

Keian, taken by Mongols, 1214, 35

Zhongdu, besieged by Mongols, 1214, 36

Zhongdu, surrendered to Mongols, 1214, May, 36

Xuancong abandoned Zhongdu and fled to Nanjing, 1214, 36

Yuerluo, Chinggis' camp, 1214, 37

Chinggis sent Samukha to invest Zhongdu, 1215 September, 37

Zhongdu, besieged by Mongols, 1214, September-1215, May, 37

Khasar campaigned in the Northeast, 1214, winter, 37

Mukhulai campaigned in the Northeast, 1214, 37

Linhuang, taken by Mongols, 1214, 37

Bienzhou, taken by Mongols, 1214, 37

Ningjiang, taken by Mongols, 1214, 37

Khasar returned to Mongolia, 1215, winter, 37

Gaozhou, taken by Mongols, 1215, 37

Yizhou, taken by Mongols, 1215, 37

Shunzhou, taken by Mongols, 1215, 37

Hete, taken by Mongols, 1215, 37

Red Coat rebellion against Jin China began in Shandong, 1215, 37

Uyer campaigned in the Northeast, 1215, 38

Longshan, taken by Mongols, 1215, 38

Xianfengchai, Shimo Mingan vs Wugulun Jingshou, Mongol victory, 1215, 38

Yongqing, Shensa vs Li Ying, Mongol victory, 2015, 38

Mukhulai's camp, 1215, 39

Chinggis returned to Mongolia, 1215, summer, 39

Chinggis sent a trade mission to Khwarizm, 1218, 42
Taiyuan, taken by Mongols, 1218, 43
Fenzhou, taken by Mongols, 1218, 43
Xizhou, taken by Mongols, 1218, 43
Fenxi, taken by Mongols, 1218, 43
Huozhou, taken by Mongols, 1218, 43
Pingyang, taken by Mongols, 1218, 43
Luan, taken by Mongols, 1218, 43
Gaoping, taken by Mongols, 1218, 43
Cezhou, taken by Mongols, 1218, 43
Otrar, Mongol trade mission seized and executed, 1218, 42

Zev remained in camp in the west, 1219, 44
Zuchi subdued the Kirghiz and campaigned into Siberia, 1219, 44
Mukhulai campaigned in Shanxi, 129, 44
Wu, taken by Mongols, 1219, 44
Keian, taken by Mongols, 1219, 44
Manzheng, Jang Ruo vs Wu Xian, Mongol victory, 1219, 44
Lanxian, taken by Mongols, 1219, 44
Xizhou, taken by Mongols, 1219, 44
Jizhou, taken by Mongols, 1219, 44
Jiangzhou, taken by Mongols, 1219, 44
Chinggis began moving west, 1219, May, 44
Chinggis camped for the summer, 1219, July, 44
Chinggis' army arrived at Otrar, 1219, November, 44
Otrar, besieged by Mongols, 1219, November-1220, February
Chinggis led the main army to Buxoro, 1219, 45
Zev moved south to Banakat, 1219, 45
Zuchi campaigned along Syr Darya River, 1219, 45

Signak, taken by Mongols, 1220, 45
Muhammad fled from Samarkand, 1220, 45
Banikat, taken by Mongols, 1220, 45
Jand, surrendered to Mongols, 1220, 45
Nurota, surrendered to Mongols, 1220, 45
Buxoro, taken by Mongols, 1220, February, 45
Otrar, taken by Mongols, 1220, February, 45
Yanikant, taken by Mongols, 1220, 45
Chinggis, Tsagadai, Ogedei, and Zev converged on Samarqand, 1220, 45
Samarqand, taken by Mongols, 1220, March 12, 45
Muhammad fled to Balkh, then Merv, 1220, 45
Chinggis camped for the summer, 1220, 46
Chinggis ordered Zev, Subeedei, and Tokhuchar to find Muhammad, 1220, 46
Balkh, surrendered to Mongols, 1220, 46

Herat, surrendered to Mongols, 1220, 46
Zaveh, taken by Mongols, 1220, 46
Neyshabur, surrendered to Mongols, 1220, 46
Tus, taken by Mongols, 1220, 46
Isfarain, taken by Mongols, 1220, 46
Asterabad, taken by Mongols, 1220, 46
Damghan, taken by Mongols, 1220, 46
Semnan, taken by Mongols, 1220, 46
Amol, taken by Mongols, 1220, 46
Ilal, taken by Mongols, 1220, 46
Ray, taken by Mongols, 1220, 46
Qazvin, taken by Mongols, 1220, 47
Zanjan, taken by Mongols, 1220, 47
Near Hamadan, Zev and Subeedei vs Khwarizm army, Mongol victory, 1220, 47
Hamadan city, surrendered to Mongols, 1220, 47
Muhammad fled to the Caspian seashore, 1220, 47
Mukhulai led another campaign against Jin China, 1220, September, 46
Daizhou, Monkhbokh vs Ge Tieqiang, Mongol victory, 1220, September, 46
Xingzhou, taken by Mongols, 1220, 46
Cizhou, taken by Mongols, 1220, 46
Zuchi advanced to Urgench, 1220, October, 47
Khiva, taken by Mongols, 1220, 47
Urgench, besieged by Mongols, 1220-1221, 47
Daming, taken by Mongols, 1220, November, 46
Zhangde, taken by Mongols, 1220, 46
Linzhou, taken by Mongols, 1220, 46
Jinan, surrendered to Mongols, 1220, 46
Dongping, besieged by Mongols, 1220-1221, 46
Huanglinggang, Mukhulai vs Wugulun Shihu, Mongol victory, 1220, 46
Jining, taken by Mongols, 1220, 46
Yanzhou, taken by Mongols, 1220, 46
Danzhou, taken by Mongols, 1220, 46
Qiuzhou, taken by Mongols, 1220, 46
Tianping, taken by Mongols, 1220, 46
Tengzhou, taken by Mongols, 1220, 46
Weihui, taken by Mongols, 1220, 46
Muhammad died on an island in the Caspian Sea, 1220, December, 47

Tsagadai joined Zuchi at the siege of Urgench, 1221, 47
Ogedei took command of the siege of Urgench, 1221, 50
Qom, taken by Mongols, 1221, February, 48
Ray, taken by Mongols, 1221, February, 48
Hamadan, surrendered to Mongols, 1221, 48

149

Aizong fled to Guide, 1233, February, 67
Nanjing surrendered to the Mongols, renamed Bian, 1233, February 26, 66
Aizong fled to Caizhou, 1233. August, 67
Guide, taken by Mongols, 1233, 67
Guyug campaigned against Puxian Wannu, 1233, 67
Yanji, taken by Mongols, 1233, 67
Seogyeong, retaken by Korea, 1233, 67
Meng Gong advanced to Caizhou, 1233 December, 67
Subeedei advanced to Caizhou, 1233 December, 67
Caizhou, besieged by Mongols, 1233-1234, 67

Aizong committed suicide, 1234 February 9, 67
Caizhou, taken by Mongols, 1234 February 9, 67
Meng Gong moved to Tanzhou, 1234, 68
Shi Songji moved to Dengzhou, 1234, 68
Zhao Gui and Quan Zucai met at Bian, 1234, 68
Caizhou, surrendered to Song China, 1234, 67
Dengzhou, surrendered to Song China, 1234, 68
Tangzhou, surrendered to Song China, 1234, 68
Tachir moved to confront Song at Henan, 1234, 68
Henan, taken by Mongols, 1234, 68
Song forces retreated from Bian, 1234, 68

Irbil, taken by Mongols, 1235, 70
Khuchu invaded Hubei, 1235, 68
Godan invaded Sichuan, 1235, 68
Cao Yuwen moved to meet Godan's invasion, 1235, 68
Mianzhou, Godan vs Cao Yuwen, Mongol defeat, 1235, 68
Tangzhou, taken by Mongols, 1235, 68
Caoyang, taken by Mongols, 1235, 68
Yingzhou, taken by Mongols, 1235, 68
Dengzhou, taken by Mongols, 1235, 68
Tangut Baatur invaded Korea, 1235, August, 69
Jeongju, taken by Mongols, 1235, 69
Gaeju, taken by Mongols, 1235, 69
Jaju, taken by Mongols, 1235, 69
Hamjong, taken by Mongols, 1235, 69
Seogyeong, taken by Mongols, 1235, 69
Yonggang, taken by Mongols, 1235, 69
Dongju, taken by Mongols, 1235, 69
Sinju, taken by Mongols, 1235, 69
Songju, taken by Mongols, 1235, 69
Ganca, taken by Mongols, 1235, winter, 70

Xiangyang, Song garrison mutinied and surrendered to Mongols, 1236, 71

Khuchu invaded Hubei, 1236, 71
Yingzhou, taken by Mongols, 1236, 71
Jingmen, taken by Mongols, 1236, 71
Jiangling, taken by Mongols, 1236, 71
Fuzhou, taken by Mongols, 1236, 71
Dean, taken by Mongols, 1236, 71
Subeedei began moving west with the main army, 1236, spring, 70
Tangut Baatur invaded Korea, 1236, April, 71
Hwangju, taken by Mongols, 1236, 71
Jipyeong, taken by Mongols, 1236, 71
Jukju, taken by Mongols, 1236, 71
Onsu, taken by Mongols, 1236, 71
Godan invaded Sichuan, 1236, summer, 71
Xingyuan, taken by Mongols, 1236, 71
Jiezhou, taken by Mongols, 1236, 71
Daan, taken by Mongols, 1236, 71
Wenzhou, taken by Mongols, 1236, 71
Lizhou, taken by Mongols, 1236, 71
Shiquan, taken by Mongols, 1236, 71
Hanzhou, taken by Mongols, 1236, 71
Chengdu, taken by Mongols, 1236, 71
Esfahan, taken by Mongols, 1236, 70
Subeedei campaigned against the Kipchaks, 1236, 70
Daeheong, taken by Mongols, 1236, 71
Subeedei vs Kipchaks, Mongol victory, 1236, 70
Bat invaded Bolgar, 1236, 72
Cuketau, taken by Mongols, 1236, 72
Bilyar, taken by Mongols, 1236, 72
Bolgar, taken by Mongols, 1236, 72
Kenek, taken by Mongols, 1236, 72
Suvar, taken by Mongols, 1236, 72
Jeonju, taken by Mongols, 1236, 71
Goransa Temple, taken by Mongols, 1236, 71
Monkh pursued Bachman, 1236, 72
Monkh vs Bachman, Mongol victory, 1236, 72

Guangzhou, resisted the Mongols, 1237, 72
Jinzhou, taken by Mongols, 1237, 72
Dazhou, taken by Mongols, 1237, 72
Huangzhou, resisted the Mongols, 1237, 72
Fuzhou, taken by Mongols, 1237, 72
Wanzhou, taken by Mongols, 1237, 72
Zizhou, taken by Mongols, 1237, 72
Anqing, resisted the Mongols, 1237, 72
Anfeng, resisted the Mongols, 1237, 72
Bat invaded Rus territories, 1237, winter, 73
Ryazan, taken by Mongols, 1237, December 21, 73

Kolomna, taken by Mongols, 1238, 73

Moskva (Moscow), taken by Mongols, 1238, 73

Vladimir, taken by Mongols, 1238, February 7, 73

Bat continued the invasion of Rus to the east, 1238, 73

Subeedei continued the invasion of Rus to the west, 1238, 73

Boroldai pursued Yuri, 1238, February, 73

Suzdal, taken by Mongols, 1238, 73

Starodub, taken by Mongols, 1238, 73

Zalessky, taken by Mongols, 1238, 73

Gorodets, taken by Mongols, 1238, 73

Ksnyatin, taken by Mongols, 1238, 73

Rostov, taken by Mongols, 1238, 73

Kashin, taken by Mongols, 1238, 73

Kostroma, taken by Mongols, 1238, 73

Dmitrov, taken by Mongols, 1238, 73

Galich, taken by Mongols, 1238, 73

Tver, taken by Mongols, 1238, 73

Yaroslavl, taken by Mongols, 1238, 73

Torzhok, taken by Mongols, 1238, March 5, 73

Sit River, Boroldai vs Yuri, Mongol victory, 1238, March 5, 73

Uglich, taken by Mongols, 1238, 73

Novgorod, submitted to Mongols, 1238, 73

Volokolamsk, taken by Mongols, 1238, 73

Vshchizh, taken by Mongols, 1238, 73

Kozelsk, taken by Mongols, 1238, 73

Chormagan split forces to invade Georgia, 1238, 75

Macnaberd, taken by Mongols, 1238, 75

Shamkor, taken by Mongols, 1238, 75

Hohanaberd, taken by Mongols, 1238, 75

Gardman, taken by Mongols, 1238, 75

Kedabek, taken by Mongols, 1238, 75

Tavush, taken by Mongols, 1238, 75

Katchen, taken by Mongols, 1238, 75

Kavazin, taken by Mongols, 1238, 75

Tuerakan, taken by Mongols, 1238, 75

Gag, taken by Mongols, 1238, 75

Gaian, taken by Mongols, 1238, 75

Lorhe, taken by Mongols, 1238, 75

Dumanise, taken by Mongols, 1238, 75

Shamshvilde, taken by Mongols, 1238, 75

Tblisi, taken by Mongols, 1238, 75

Rusudan fled as Mongols approached, 1238, 75

Tangut Baatur invaded Korea, 1238, 74

Xiangyang, recovered by Song China, 1238, 74

Kuizhou, resisted the Mongols, 1238, 74

Luzhou, resisted the Mongols, 1238, 74

Berkh campaigned against the Cumans, 1238, 75

Monkh and Khadan campaigned against the Alans, 1238, 75

Shiban and Buri campaigned to Crimea, 1238, 75

Berkh vs Koten (Cumans), Mongol victory, 128, 75

Maghas, taken by Mongols, 1238, 75

Soldaia, taken by Mongols, 1238, 75

Koten fled to Hungary with his followers, 1238, 75

Sangju, taken by Mongols, 1238, 74

Donggyeong, taken by Mongols, 1238, 74

Chormagan campaigned in Armenia, 1239, 76

Hrashkaberd, taken by Mongols, 1239, 76

Pereyaslavl, taken by Mongols, 1239, March 3, 77

Ani, taken by Mongols, 1239, 76

Chongqing, resisted the Mongols, 1239, 76

Wanzhou, taken by Mongols, 1239, 76

Dazhou, taken by Mongols, 1239, 76

Daya Camp, Mongols vs Song, Song victory, 1239, 76

Kars, taken by Mongols, 1239, 76

Kuizhou, resisted the Mongols, 1239, 76

Shizhou, resisted the Mongols, 1239, 76

Hlukhiv, taken by Mongols, 1239, 77

Novgorod-Seversk, taken by Mongols, 1239, 77

Snovsk, taken by Mongols, 1239, 77

Chernihiv, taken by Mongols, 1239 October 18, 77

Doorda Darkhan led expedition to Tibet, 1240, 77

Bat moved against Kyyiv (Kiev), 1240 November, 78

Monkh supported the invasion of Kyyiv with the advance force, 1240, 78

Kyyiv, taken by Mongols, 1240, December 6, 78

Kolodyazhin, Bat vs Halych, Mongol victory, 1241, 78

Kamaniets, Bat vs Halych, Mongol victory, 1241, 78

Iziaslavl, Bat vs Halych, Mongol victory, 1241, 78

Baidar and Ord advanced against Volodomyr, 1241, 78

Bat advanced against Halych, 1241, January, 78

Halych, taken by Mongols, 1241, 78

Volodymyr, taken by Mongols, 1241, 78

Bat invaded Hungary with his main force, 1241, 78

Baidar and Ord invaded Poland, 1241, 78

Boroldai supported invasion of Hungary, 1241, 78

Bujek supported invasion of Hungary, 1241, 78

Khadan supported invasion of Hungary, 1241, 78

Shiban supported invasion of Hungary, 1241, 78

Verecke Pass, Bat vs Hungarians, Mongol victory, 1241, 78

Lubin, taken by Mongols, 1241, 78

Bibliography

Allsen, Thomas.T. "Guard and Government in the Reign of the Grand Qan Möngke, 1251-59." *Harvard Journclal of Asiatic Studies* 46, no. 2 (1986): 495-521.

———. "Prelude to the Western Campaigns: Mongol Military Operations in Volga-Ural Region 1217-1237." *Archivum Eurasiae Mediiaevi*. 3 (1983): 5-24.

Amitai, Reuven. "Mongol Raids into Palestine (A.D. 1260 and 1300)." *Journal of the Royal Asiatic Society of Great Britain and Ireland/* 2 (1987): 236-55.

Atwood, Christopher Pratt. *Encyclopedia of Mongolia and the Mongolian Empire*. New York, NY: Facts On File, 2004.

Aung-Thwin, Michael Arthur. *Pagan : The Origins of Modern Burma*. Honolulu: University of Hawaii Press, 1985.

Baiarsaikhan, D. *Mongolchuud*. Ulaanbaatar Khot : Monsudar Khėvlėliin Gazar, 2016.

Bazarg*ur, D., and D. *Enkhba*i*ar. *Chinggis Khaan (*Cinggis Qayan) : Historic-Geographic Atlas*. Ulaan-baatar: Cartographic Enterprise of the State Administration of Geodesy and Cartography, 1997.

Bazilevich, Konstantin Vasilevich. *Atlas Istorii Sssr*. 1951.

Biran, Michal. *The Empire of the Qara Khitai in Eurasian History : Between China and the Islamic World, Cambridge Studies in Islamic Civilization*. Cambridge, UK ; New York: Cambridge University Press, 2005.

———. "Il-Khanate Empire." In *The Encyclopedia of Empire*. edited by John M. MacKenzie. location Hoboken, New Jersey: John Wiley & Sons, Ltd., 2016.

———. "Kitan Migrations in Eurasia (10th–14th Centuries)." *Journal of Central Eurasian Studies*. 3 (2012): 85-108.

———. *Qaidu and the Rise of the Independent Mongol State in Central Asia*. Surrey: Curzon, 1997.

Bosworth, Clifford Edmund. *The New Islamic Dynasties : A Chronological and Genealogical Manual. Enl. and updated*. New York: Columbia University Press, 1996.

Boyle, John Andrew. *The Cambridge History of Iran. Vol. 5, Saljuq and Mongol periods*. Cambridge University Press.2008.

———. "The Mongol Commanders in Afghanistan and India According to the Tabaqāt-I Nāsirī of Jūzjānī." *Islamic Studies* 2, no. 2 (1963): 235-48.

Buell, Paul D. "Early Mongol Expansion in Western Siberia and Turkestan (1207-1219): A Reconstruction." *Central Asiatic Journal* 36, no. 1/2 (1992): 1-32.

———. "Kalmyk Tanggaci People: Thoughts on the Mechanics and Impact of Mongol Expansion." *Mongolian Studies* 6 (1980): 41-59.

Campbell, Anthony. *Assassins of Alamut*. [Place of publication not identified]: Lulu Com, 2008.

Chi-Yun, Chang. *Historical Atlas of China*. Yangmingshan, Taiwan: Chinese Culture University Press, 1980.

Cleaves, Francis Woodman "The Biography of Bayan of the Bārin in the Yüan Shih." *Harvard Journal of Asiatic Studies* 19, no. 3/4 (1956): 185-303.

———. *The Secret History of the Mongols : For the First Time Done into English out of the Original Tongue and Provided with an Exegetical Commentary.* Cambridge, Mass.; London, England: Published for the Harvard-Yenching Institute by Harvard University Press, 1982.

de Rachewiltz, Igor. *In the Service of the Khan : Eminent Personalities of the Early Mongol-Yüan Period (1200-1300), Asiatische Forschungen,.* Wiesbaden: Harrassowitz, 1993.

———. "Personnel and Personalities in North China in the Early Mongol Period." *Journal of the Economic and Social History of the Orient* 9, no. 1/2 (1966): 88-144.

———. *The Secret History of the Mongols : A Mongolian Epic Chronicle of the Thirteenth Century.* 3 vols, Brill's Inner Asian Library. Leiden ; Boston: Brill, 2004.

Engel, Josef, and Bayerischer Schulbuch-Verlag. *Grosser Historischer Weltatlas.* 4., überarbeitete und erw. Aufl. ed. München: Bayerischer Schulbuch-Verlag, 1981.

Franke, Herbert, and Denis Twitchett. *The Cambridge History of China. Vol. 6 : Alien Regimes and Border States, 907-1368.* Cambridge: Cambridge University Press, 1995.

Freeman-Grenville, G. S. P., S. C. Munro-Hay, and Lorraine Kessel. *Historical Atlas of Islam.* New York: Continuum International Pub. Group, 2002.

Golden, P. B. ""I Will Give the People Unto Thee": The Činggisid Conquests and Their Aftermath in The Turkic World." *Journal of the Royal Asiatic Society* 10, no. 1 (2000): 21-41.

Grousset, René. *The Empire of the Steppes; a History of Central Asia.* New Brunswick, N.J.,: Rutgers University Press, 1970.

Haig, Wolseley. *The Cambridge History of India.* III, III. Cambridge: University Press, 1928.

Halperin, Charles J. "The Missing Golden Horde Chronicles and Historiography in the Mongol Empire." *Mongolian Studies* 23 (2000): 1-15.

Hanguk Kyowon Taehakkyo. Department of History Education. *Atlas of Korean History.* English ed. Singapore: Published and distributed by Stallion Press, 2008.

Henthorn, William E. *Korea: The Mongol Invasions.* Leiden,: E.J. Brill, 1963.

Herrmann, Albert, Norton Sydney Ginsburg, and Paul Wheatley. *An Historical Atlas of China.* New ed. Chicago,: Aldine Pub. Co., 1966.

Holt, P. M., Ann K. S. Lambton, and Bernard Lewis. *The Cambridge History of Islam.* Cambridge ; New York: Cambridge University Press, 1977.

Jackson, Peter. "The Dissolution of the Mongol Empire." *Central Asiatic Journal* 22, no. 3/4 (1978): 186-244.

———. "Jalāl Al-Dīn, the Mongols, and the Khwarazmian Conquest of the Panjāb and Sind." *Iran* 28 (1990): 45-54.

———. *The Mongols and the Latin West : 1221-1410.* Harlow: Longman, 2004.

Kennedy, Hugh, Marc Bel, and Peter van der Donck. *An Historical Atlas of Islam = Atlas Historique De L'islam.* Leiden; Boston: Brill, 2002.

Kim, Hodong. "The Unity of the Mongol Empire and Continental Exchanges over Eurasia." *Journal of Central Eurasian Studies* 1 (2009): 15-42.

Krawulsky, Dorothea. "The Testament of Cingiz Khan." In *The Mongol Ilkhans and Their Vizier Rashid Al-Din*. Frankfurt am Main; Berlin; Bern [etc.]: P. Mang, 2011.

Lane, George. "The Dali Stele." In *Horizons of the World: Festschrift for Isenbike Togan / Hududü'l-Alem: İsenbike Togan'a Armağan*, edited by Nurten Kilic-Schubel and Evrim Binbash. Istanbul: Ithaki Press, 2011.

———. "Early Mongol Rule in Thirteenth-Century Iran: A Persian Renaissance." In *Studies in the History of Iran and Turkey*, edited by Carole Hillenbrand. Edinburgh: University of Edinburgh, 2003.

Le Strange, G. *Baghdad : During the Abbasid Caliphate*. New York: Cosim Classics, 2011.

———. *The Lands of the Eastern Caliphate*. S.l.: s.n., 1966.

Lind, John. "Mongol Invasions of Russia." In *The Encyclopedia of War*, edited by Gordon Martel: Blackwell Publishing Ltd., 2012.

Luc Kwanten. "The Career of Muqali: A Reassessment." *Bulletin of Sung and Yüan Studies*, no. 14 (1978): 31-38.

———. *Imperial Nomads : A History of Central Asia, 500-1500*. Philadelphia: University of Pennsylvania Press, 1979.

Magocsi, Paul R., and Geoffrey J. Matthews. *Historical Atlas of East Central Europe*. 1st pbk., with corrections. ed, A History of East Central Europe ; V. 1. Seattle: University of Washington Press, 1995.

———. *Ukraine, a Historical Atlas*. Toronto ; Buffalo: University of Toronto Press, 1985.

Man, John. *The Mongol Empire : Genghis Khan, His Heirs and the Founding of Modern China*. 2015.

Martin, Henry Desmond. *The Rise of Chingis Khan and His Conquest of North China*. New York,: Octagon Books, 1971.

May, Timothy Michael. "Chormaqan Noyan: The First Mongol Military Governor in the Middle East." Thesis, Indiana University, 1996.

———. *The Mongol Art of War : Chinggis Khan and the Mongol Military System*. Yardley, Penn.: Westholme, 2007.

———. *The Mongol Empire : A Historical Encyclopedia*. 2017.

———. "Mongol Empire: Chormaquan and the Mongol Conquest of the Middle East." http://www.historynet.com/mongol-empire-chormaquan-and-the-mongol-conquest-of-the-middle-east.htm.

———. "A Mongol-Ismâ'îlî Alliance?: Thoughts on the Mongols and Assassins." *Journal Of The Royal Asiatic Society*. (2016).

McLynn, Frank. *Genghis Khan : His Conquests, His Empire, His Legacy*. Da Capo Press, 2015.

Michell, Robert, Nevill Forbes, and A. A. Shakhmatov. *The Chronicle of Novgorod, 1016-1471*. Charleston, SC: BiblioLife, 2010.

Minhaj Siraj, Juzjani, and H. G. Raverty. Tabakat-I-Nasiri : *A General History of the Muhammadan Dynasties of Asia, Including Hindustan from A.H. 194 (810 A.D.) to A.H. 658 (1260 A.D.) and the Irruption of the Infidel Mughals into Islam*. Kolkata: The Asiatic Society, 2010.

Nelson, John Carl. "Interactive Historical Atlas of the World since 3000bce." Alexandria, VA: World History Maps, Inc., 2013.

Nicolle, David, and Richard Hook. *The Mongol Warlords : Genghis Khan, Kublai Khan, Hülegü, Tamerlane*. Poole, Dorset; New York, N.Y.: Firebird Books ; Distributed in the United States by Sterling Pub. Co., 1990.

Pluvier, Jan M. *Historical Atlas of South-East Asia*. New York: E.J. Brill, 1995.

Pow, Lindsey Stephen. "Deep Ditches and Well-Built Walls: A Reappraisal of the Mongol Withdrawal from Europe in 1242." Thesis, University of Calgary, 2012.

Qu Da-Feng. "A Study of Jebe's Expedition to Tung Ching." *Acta Orientalia Academiae Scientiarum Hungaricae* 51, no. 1/2 (1998): 171-77.

Qu Dafeng and Liu Jianyi. "On Some Problems Concerning Jochi's Lifetime." *Central Asiatic Journal* 42, no. 2 (1998): 283-90.

Rady, Martyn C., László Veszprémy, János M. Bak, *Notarius Anonymus Belae Regis, and Rogerius. Anonymus and Master Roger. : Anonymi Bele Regis Notarii Gesta Hungarorum = the Deeds of the Hungarians*. Budapest; New York: Central European University Press, 2010.

Raphael, Kate. "Mongol Siege Warfare on the Banks of the Euphrates and the Question of Gunpowder (1260-1312)." *Journal of the Royal Asiatic Society*. Third Series 19, no. 3 (2009): 355-70.

Riley-Smith, Jonathan Simon Christopher, and Swanston Graphics Limited. *The Atlas of the Crusades*. New York: Facts on File, 1991.

Rossabi, Morris. *Khubilai Khan : His Life and Times*. Berkeley: University of California Press, 1988.

Ryavec, Karl. *A Historical Atlas of Tibet*. Chicago; London: The University of Chicago Press, 2015.

Saunders, J. J. *The History of the Mongol Conquests*. Philadelphia: University of Pennsylvania Press, 2001.

Schwarz, Henry G. "Mongolia at 800: The State and Nation since Chinggis Khan." *Inner Asia*, 8, no. 2 (2006): 151-61.

Sen, Tansen. "The Formation of Chinese Maritime Networks to Southern Asia, 1200-1450." *Journal of the Economic and Social History of the Orient* 49, no. 4 (2006): 421-53.

Shen, Qianfang. "The Opening of the Roads from Yunnan to Huguang Province." *Asian Social Science* 6, no. 9 (2010): 55-58.

Sinor, Denis. *The Cambridge History of Early Inner Asia*. Cambridge [Cambridgeshire] ; New York: Cambridge University Press, 1990.

———. "The Inner Asian Warriors." *Journal of the American Oriental Society* 101, no. 2 (1981): 133-44.

———. "The Mongols in the West." *Journal of Asian History* 33, no. 1 (1999): 1-44.

Smith, John Masson Jr. "Ayn Jālūt: Mamlūk Sucess or Mongol Failure?" *Harvard Journal of Asiatic Studies* 44, no. 2 (1984): 307-45.

Sverdrup, Carl Fredrik. *The Mongol Conquests: The Military Operations of Genghis Khan and Sübe'etei*. Solihull: Helion and Company, 2017.

Tatár, Sarolta. "Roads Used by the Mongols into Hungary, 1241-1242." In *Proceedings of the 10th International Congress of Mongolists*, 334-41. Ulaanbaatar, 2012.

Teslia, Ivan, Evhen Tiutko, and Lubomyr Roman Wynar. *Istorychnyi Atlas Ukraïny*. Montreal* ; New York: Ukraïnske istorychne tovarystvo, 1980.

Tserensodnom, D., and D. Tomortogoo. *Mongolyn Nuuts Tovchoo : Erdem Shinzhilgeenii Orchuulga, Tailbar*. Ulaanbaatar: Shinzhlekh Ukhaany Akademiin Khel Zokhiolyn Khureelen, 2000.

Twitchett, Denis Crispin. *The Cambridge History of China Vol. 5, Part 1, part 1, The Sung dynasty and its precursors, 907-1279*. Cambridge: Cambridge University Press, 2009.

Vernadsky, George. *A History of Russia. Vol. III,* New Haven: Yale University Press, 1970.

Verschuer, Zuikei Shuho and Charlotte von. "Japan's Foreign Relations 1200 to 1392 A.D.: A Translation from "Zenrin Kokuhōki"." *Monumenta Nipponica* 57, no. 4 (2002): 413-45.

Walters, C. C. "Sketch Map of the Great Raid by Chepé & Subutai, 1220-1224." Document in the Library of Congress.

Weatherford, J. McIver. *Genghis Khan and the Making of the Modern World*. 1st ed. New York: Crown, 2004.

Whiting, Marvin C. *Imperial Chinese Military History: 8000 BC-1912 Ad*. San Jose: Writer's Club Press, 2002.

Wieczynski, Joseph L., and George N. Rhyne. *The Modern Encyclopedia of Russian and Soviet History*, Academic International Reference Series. Gulf Breeze, Fla.: Academic International Press, 1976.

Willey, Peter. *The Castles of the Assassins*. London, 1963.

Woods, John E. "A Note on the Mongol Capture of Isfahān." *Journal of Near Eastern Studies* 36, no. 1 (1977): 49-51.

Wright, David Curtis. "Navies in the Mongol Yuan Conquest of Southern Song China, 1274-1279." *Mongolian Studies* 29 (2007): 207-16.

Wylie, Turrell V. . "The First Mongol Conquest of Tibet Reinterpreted." *Harvard Journal of Asiatic Studies* 37, no. 1 (1977): 103-33.

Yamamura, Kozo. *The Cambridge History of Japan*. Vol. 3 : Medieval Japan. Cambridge: Cambridge University Press, 1990.

Zhongguo jun shi shi bian xie zu. *Zhongguo Li Dai Zhan Zheng Nian Biao*. 2 2. Beijing: Jie fang jun chu ban she, 2003.

Zhongguo ren min ge ming jun shi bo wu guan., and Xing qiu di tu chu ban she. *Zhongguo Zhan Zheng Shi Di Tu Ji = Zhongguo Zhanzhengshi Dituji*. Beijing: Xing qiu di tu chu ban she, 2007.

Zimonyi, István "The Volga Bulghars between Wind and Water (1220—1236)." *Acta Orientalia Academiae Scientiarum Hungaricae* 46, no. 2/3 (1992/93): 347-55.

https://en.wikipedia.org

https://mn.wikipedia.org

https://translate.google.com

Notes

List of Abbreviations used in the notes

AKH   Hanguk Kyowon Taehakkyo. Department of History Education. *Atlas of Korean History*. English ed. Singapore: Published and distributed by Stallion Press, 2008.

CHC5 Twitchett, Denis Crispin. *The Cambridge History of China Vol. 5, Part 1, The Sung dynasty and its precursors, 907-1279*. Cambridge: Cambridge University Press, 2009.

CHC6 Franke, Herbert, and Denis Twitchett. *The Cambridge History of China. Vol. 6 : Alien Regimes and Border States, 907-1368*. Cambridge: Cambridge University Press, 1995.

CHI5 Boyle, John Andrew. *The Cambridge History of Iran. Vol. 5, Saljuq and Mongol periods*. Cambridge University Press.2008.

NB   Zhongguo jun shi shi" bian xie, zu. *Zhongguo Li Dai Zhan Zheng Nian Biao*. 2 2. Beijing: Jie fang jun chu ban she, 2003.

SH   de Rachewiltz, Igor. *The Secret History of the Mongols : A Mongolian Epic Chronicle of the Thirteenth Century*. 3 vols, Brill's Inner Asian Library. Leiden ; Boston: Brill, 2004.

ZZ   Zhongguo ren min ge ming jun shi bo wu guan., and Xing qiu di tu chu ban she. *Zhongguo Zhan Zheng Shi Di Tu Ji = Zhongguo Zhanzhengshi Dituji*. Beijing: Xing qiu di tu chu ban she, 2007.

Temujin

1, Weatherford, 14-17, 28-29.
2, Bazargur, 10-11.
3, Bazargur, 12-13.
4, Bazargur, 12-13.
5, Bazargur, 12-15.
6, Bazargur, 16-17.
7, Bazargur, 18-19; SH, 104-113.
8, Bazargur, 28-21.
9, Bazargur, 22-23; SH 129.
10, Bazargur, 24-25.
11, Bazargur, 24-25; SH, 132-133. The title of King, Wang in Chinese, became Ong in Mongolian. Tooril thereafter also known as Ong Khan.
12, Bazargur, 24-25; SH, 132, 136.
13, Bazargur, 26-27; SH, 141-144.
14, Bazargur, 26-29.
15, Bazargur, 30-31; SH, 378.
16, Bazargur, 26-27; SH, 157.
17, Bazargur, 30-31; SH, 81-82.
18, Bazargur, 32-33.
19, Bazargur, 32-33; SH, 185.

20, Bazargur, 34-35; SH, 189-196, 1046. Taibokh was also known at Tayang Khan.
21, Bazargur, 34-35; SH 189-196, 1046.
21, Bazargur, 36-37.
22, Martin, 94-95; SH, 1046.
23, SH, 133-141.

Chinggis

1, Bazargur, 34-35; SH, 1047. The sequence of this campaign in the *Secret History* places it around 1199, The chronology according to de Rachewiltz, however, puts it in 1206 which is more logical. There would have been no reason for Temujin to attack Buirug until after the Naimans had joined Jamukha's coalition.
2, Martin, 102-103; SH, 1047.
3, SH, 239, 1047.
4, Bazargur, 36-37; SH, 1047-48.
5, Martin, 116-118.
6, Martin, 118-119; SH, 1048; map based on Google Earth, size of outer wall is conjectural.
7, Martin, 129-133.

8, Bazargur, 38-39; SH, 235, 1048. Khubilai Noyon distinguishes him from Khubilai, son of Tului.

9, Martin, 164-137, 146.

10, Martin, 137-144, 146-147.

11, Martin, 145-146. Qu Dafeng.

12, Martin, 150-152. Qu Dafeng.

13, Martin, 155-157. Withdrawal to favorable grasslands was a standard Mongol practice after a campaign and would be seen many times again. The Mongol conquests unfolded as an intermittent series of what Timothy May has described as "tidal waves." There were sometimes long pauses between campaigns and frequent withdrawals from areas that had been conquered. Many places had to be retaken several times. When these withdrawals happened to coincide with the death of a Great Khan, many assumed that the Mongols were required to return to their homeland to choose a successor. This was never the case.

14, Martin, 158-160.

15, Martin, 160-164.

16, Martin, 164-167.

17, Martin, 168-170; city map based on Chang, 5, superimposed on Google Earth, rivers from Digital Chart of the World.

18, Martin, 171-174.

19, Martin, 174, 203-207.

20, Martin, 174-178; city map based on Chang, 5, superimposed on Google Earth, rivers from Digital Chart of the World.

21, Martin, 176, 178, 207-210, 218-217.

22, Martin, 185-186.

23, Martin, 211-212.

24, Martin, 184-187.

25, Martin, 212-216.

26, Martin, 187-190.

27, McLynn, 253; Bazargur, 38-39.

28, Bazargur, 38-39; SH, 1049.

29, Martin, 216-217; Henworth, 14-19, 31-41.

30, Martin, 241-244.

31, Bazargur, 36-37; SH 1049-50.

32, Martin, 245-248.

33, Bazargur, 38-39; SH 1050.

34, Martin, 248-250.

35, Martin, 236-237; SH, 182-188, 923; Krawulsky, 19-28. The Secret History contains a story that before Chinggis left for the west, the issue of succession was raised. After Tsagadai questioned Zuchi's paternity, Ogedei was chosen. de Rachewiltz and Krawulsky maintain that this was a later interpolation used to justify the ascendency of Ogedei, and then Tului's line, and that Chinggis did not designate a successor. It was not the Mongol custom for a leader to choose his own successor. The fact that two years passed before Ogedei was confirmed as Great Khan further supports this view.

36, McLynn, 269-277.

37, McLynn, 277-280.

38, McLynn, 284-287.

39, Martin, 250-253, 258-259.

40, McLynn, 290-295; Sverdrup 155, 160. Sverdrup states that Tsagadai and Ogedei were sent to Urgench and Zuchi was to support them.

41, McLynn, 287-289.

42, Walters, map.

43, Mc Lynn, 296-307; While Tului's campaign in Khurasan was certainly destructive, it could not have been the total annihilation described in some accounts. For example, the city of Merv, in which Tului is described as killing every living person, was still able to stage a rebellion a few months later.

44, McLynn 308-310.

45, McLynn, 319-328. McLynn describes a difficult crossing of the Caucasus Mountains in the winter after Derbent. However Derbent is on the coast of the Caspian Sea, well north and east of the mountain crest. To move north, Zev and Subeedei would have simply followed the coast with no difficulty.

46, McLynn, 312-318.

47, Martin, 260-268.

48, McLynn, 328-330. Location of these battles not determined.

49, Martin, 268-281.

50, McLynn, 339-343.

51, Martin, 276-277.

52, Martin, 271-273. Luc, The Career of Mukhulai.

53, McLynn, 360-362.

54, Jackson, 34.

55, Martin, 277-278.

56, Martin, 279-281.

57, Martin, 289-295; Sverdrup, 97-100.

58, Martin, 295-302.

59, McLynn, 376-379; SH, 979-983.

60, CHI5, 330; May, Chormaqan Governor, 19.

Ogedei

1, Grousset, 254-255.
2, CHI5, 330; May, Chormaqan Governor 19; Woods 49.
3, de Rachewiltz, Service, 20-21.
4, Allsen, Prelude.
5, May, Chormaqan Governor, 20-21; CHI5, 368.
6, McLynn, 396; Sverdrup 228-232.
7, May, Chormaqan, 27-28; CHI5 334-336.
8, CHI5, 336.
9, May, Chormaqan Governor, 28-31; CHI5 334-336.
10, Henthorn, 61-65. AKH, 83-84.
11, Chang, 107; Sverdrup 240-243.
12, Chang, 107; Sverdrup 243-256.
13, Henthorn, 67-74. AKH, 83-84.
14, CHC6, 263-264; city map based on Chang, 8, superimposed on Google Earth, rivers from Digital Chart of the World.
15, CHC5, Chang, 107.
16, Henthorn, 100; Wikipedia, Guyuk.
17, CHC6, 264, 372.
18, CHI5, 864; ZZ, 121.
19, Henthorn, 77-78. AKH, 83-84.
20, Jackson, 105.
21, McLynn, 436.
22, May, Chormaquan Conquest.
23, CHC5, 864; ZZ, 121.
24, Henthorn, 102-103. AKH, 83-84.
25, McLynn, 433-436.
26, CHC5, 865; ZZ, 121.
27, McLynn, 438-441.
28, McLynn, 441-442.
29, CHC5, 866; ZZ, 121.
30, Henthorn, 102-103; AKH, 83-84.
31, May, Chormaquan Conquest,
32, McLynn, 442.
33, CHC5, 866; ZZ, 121.
34, May, Chormaquan Conquest,
35, McLynn, 443.
36, Wylie, 110-111, Ryavec, Map 22.
37, McLynn, 444-446.
38, McLynn, 448-457; slovak-republic.org/history.
39, McLynn, 458-474; slovak-republic.org/history.
40, McLynn, 475-479; slovak-republic.org/history. According to some, Bat was fearful about crossing the frozen Danube River. This seems unlikely because he had already crossed the Volga, Don, and Dnieper Rivers in winter.
41, CHC5, 867; ZZ, 121.
42, Boyle, 240; Haig, 62-63; Jackson 105.

Guyug

1, Atwood, 544; Grousset, 268-269. Temuge attempted to claim the title of Great Khan after Ogedei's death but was not successful. He was tried by Ord and Monkh, and executed by Guyug in 1246.
2, McLynn, 472-479. 3, CHC5, 867; CHC6, 383.
4, Atwood, 321;McLynn, 481.
5, Vernadsky 142-143.
6, CHC5, 867; CHC6, 383.
7, Ryavec, Map 22.
8, Boyle, 239; Haig, 65; Jackson, 106.
9, CHC6, 388; NB, 175.
10, Henworth, 106.
11, Grousset, 272; CHC6, 389.

Monkh

1, Atwood, 418-419; Grousset, 872-874.
2, Vernadsky, 148.
3, Atwood, 63; Nicolle, 104; Rossabi, 44-45.
4, Ryavec, Map 22.
5, CHI5, 342.
6, CHC5, 407,869; Lane, Dali, 14.
7, Henthorn, 112; AKH, 83-84.
8, CHI5, 341; Boyle, Juvaini, 611-612.
9, CHC5, 407,869; Lane, Dali, 14.
10, Henthorn, 127; AKH, 83-84. Did not find sources for a year by year breakdown of these campaigns.
11, CHI5, 341-342; Boyle, Juvaini, 613-618. Khulegu's progress through Persia was more in the way of a ceremonial tour rather than an invasion.
12, CHI5, 343-344; Boyle, Juvaini, 618-634; Willey, 162-168. Lammasar held out for a year. Kurshah was initially well treated and sent to Mongolia to make his submission to Monkh. However on the return journey, Monkh ordered him and all the other Ismailis who had surrendered to be killed.
13, CHI5, 346.
14, CHC5, 407,869; Lane, Dali, 14.
15, Wikipedia, Daniel of Galicia.
16, Pluvier, 17, Map 10; Lane, Dali, 21-23.
17, CHI5, 346-348, Nicolle, 130.

18, CHI5, 348-349; Nicolle, 130-132; city map based on Kennedy, 28, superimposed on Google Earth, rivers from Digital Chart of the World. Accounts of two million killed at Baghdad are wildly exaggerated. The city was a shadow of its former self and it is doubtful that there were two million people in all of Iraq at this time (themasites.pbl.nl/tridion/en/themasites/hyde/).

19, Chang, 107; ZZ, 121.

20, Haig, 72; Jackson 108.

21, Chang, 107; ZZ, 121.

22, Vernadsky, 158.

23, Chang, 107; ZZ, 121.

24, ZZ, 121; detail map based on ZZ, 121, superimposed on Google Earth, rivers from Digital Chart of the World.

Khubilai

1, Rossabi, 48-49; Chang, 107; ZZ, 121.

2, Vernadsky, 158.

3, CHI5, 350-351; Nicolle, 112.

4, CHI5, 351; Nicolle, 112-113; Amitai 237-239.

5, Rossabi, 51-53.

6, Amitai, 27-52; CHI5, 351; Nicolle, 114-117. The battle of Ain Jalut has assumed mythic dimensions as the place where the Mongols were stopped. The Mongols were never stopped, they stopped because of their own internal situation. This minor defeat of a small force had no effect. Khulegu sent another small army later in the year. Khulegu did not come back with his full force because of the revolt of Mosul, the war with Berkh, and the loss of Mongol unity.

7, Rossabi, 56-58; de Rachewiltz, Service, 485-486.

8, Rossabi, 57-59.

9, CHI5 354; Nicolle, 120.

10, NB, 21. Details of movements for these actions not determined.

11, Rossabi, 60-61.

12, Rossabi, 64-65; CHC6, 426.

13, CHI5, 352-353, Amitai, 79-80.

14, CHI5, 353-354.

15, Rossabi, 60-61. Many works attribute Arigbokh's defeat to being cut off from sources of grain and weapons from the settled areas. This seems strange since Mongol armies did not need supplies of grain and had their own weapons. Kharkhorum itself needed supplies but it belonged to Khubilai already in the second year of the conflict. It was not a lack of supplies but a lack of supporters.

16, Atwood, 202.

17, Atwood, 202.

18, CHI5, 356; Atwood, 202.

19, NB, 21.

20, Biran, Qaidu, 22; Dicosimo, Warfare, 178-199.

21, NB, 21.

22, Biran, Qaidu, 23-25

23, Nicolle, 88; Rossabi 84; city map based on Google Earth, rivers from Digital Chart of the World.

24, Nicolle, 88-89; Rossabi 85; city map based on Google Earth, rivers from Digital Chart of the World.

25, NB, 21

26, Dicosimo, Warfare, 178-199, CHI5, 360.

27, Henworth, 162, 173-175; AKH, 84.

28, Rossabi, 107-108.

29, Nicolle, 89; Rossabi 85; city map based on Google Earth, rivers from Digital Chart of the World. Khubilai must have requested the Muslim engineers much earlier in the siege since it would have taken many months for the request to reach Persia, for the engineers to prepare and travel back, and to construct the trebuchets and assemble the projectiles.

30, CHI5, 131-140; AKH, 84.

31, de Rachewiltz, Service, 388-389; Cleves, 209-216; Chang, 107; ZZ, 121.

32, de Rachewiltz, Service, 390-391; Cleves, 216-225; Chang, 107; ZZ, 121.

33, de Rachewiltz, Service, 391-392; Cleves, 225-230; Chang, 107; ZZ, 121.

34, Biran, 38-39.

35, de Rachewiltz, Service, 392-393; Chang, 107; ZZ, 121.

36, de Rachewiltz, Service, 394-395; Cleves, 235-246; Chang, 106; ZZ, 121.

37, Chang, 107; ZZ, 121.

38, Biran, 38-41; de Rachewiltz, Service, 397-398.

39, Chang, 107; ZZ, 121; Pluvier, 18.

40, Amitai, 168-178; CHI5, 361.

41, Chang, 107; ZZ, 121.

Wars and Expeditions

1, Amitai, 183-201.

2, CHC6, 482; Rossabi, 208-212; AKH, 84.

3, Pluvier, 17.

4, Wikipedia, Mongol Invasion of Burma.

5, Biran, 43.

6, Ryavec, Map 22; Biran, 45.

7, Haig, 82; Jackson 117.

8, Vernadsky, 181. Route of Hungarian army and site
    of battle not determined.

9, Pluvier, 17.

10, Wikipedia, Mongol Invasion of Burma.

11, CHC6, 489; Atwood, 401. Locations of these
    battles not determined.

12, Pluvier, 17.

13, Vernadsky, 182.

14, CHI5, 370. Location of these battles not deter-
    mined.

15, CHI5, 370.

16, Biran, 46-47.

17, Haig, 95; Jackson, 118. Movements of Delhi Sul-
    tan Firuz not determined.

18, Biran, 48-49.

19, Pluvier, 16.

20, CHI5, 372-6; Biran 58-59.

21, Haig, 102; Jackson, 11/-222.

22, Raphael, 638.

23, Biran, 60.

24, Biran, 52-54.

25, Haig, 108-109; Jackson 222.

26, Raphael, 638.

Name and Subject Index

As noted in the introduction, The romanization of foreign names is a difficult problem. Many countries have adopted new systems in recent years, but a lot of the sources used the older systems. I have tried to conform to the most current usage as best I could. I apologize for any inadvertent errors.

Mongolian names are written according to modern Mongolian spelling, using Mongol Wikipedia and a recent Mongol translation of the *Secret History* as guides, converted from the Cyrillic alphabet. Alternate spellings are included in the Index in parentheses, eg Chinggis (Genghis).

Chinese names are written using the Pinyin system. Place names are the names used at the time. Corresponding modern names of major cities are shown in the index.

Korean names are written using the Revised Romanization system. Place names are the names used at the time. Corresponding modern names of major cities are shown in the index.

Place names in the west are written using their modern names except for Constantinople.

Geographic names (cities, mountains, rivers, lakes, etc) are written using current spelling as in the National Geographic Atlas of the World. Abbreviations are used for Lake/L, River/R. The more widely known English name is sometimes shown in parentheses for some of the more famous names, eg: Halab (Aleppo), Chang (Yangtze) R. Geographic names are not included in the index unless they are mentioned in the text.

Made in the USA
Las Vegas, NV
17 November 2023

81006197R00117